Potawatomi Tears
&
Petticoat Pioneers
More of the Romance
of Michigan's Past

For Eleanor

I hope you enjoy!

Larry B Massie

William Nowlin included a view of his family's lonely cabin amidst the big trees near Dearborn in 1834 in his autobiography, *The Bark Covered House.*

Potawatomi Tears
&
Petticoat Pioneers
More of the Romance
of Michigan's Past

by Larry B. Massie

The Priscilla Press
Allegan Forest, Michigan
1992

Cover by Judi Miller Morris
Title Graphic by Devon Blackwood
Printing by Bookcrafters, Chelsea, MI

ISBN: Soft Cover 0-9626408-3-2
Hard Cover 0-9626408-4-0

First Edition—September 1992

For my mother, June Massie, who taught me to laugh.

In 1945, two beauties of a similar vintage posed together. My father's robin-egg blue 1932 Ford Roadster eventually wore out. The gal, June Massie, has gotten better each passing year.

TABLE OF CONTENTS

PREFACE

We had hiked for three or four miles along the overgrown old road that snaked through the Allegan State Forest, wondering about the moccasin clad feet which had first beat a path here, breathing deep the white pine scented breeze, pointing out deer and wild turkey tracks and the bone white trunk of a huge sycamore, letting but little talk break nature's mood. Reaching our destination, we stood atop a steep sand bluff. A hundred feet below rippled the Kalamazoo River, lazily meandering into the distance.

Swallows darted from nests in the sand bank to perform their aerial acrobatics and a kingfisher swooped low across the water. At the crumbling brink of the cliff I found bark-like Woodland pottery shards and nearby lay a handful of flint chips, residue of a ancient toolmaker's worksite. I could all but feel the presence of the aboriginal Michiganders who had long ago chosen this site to live and love and I could almost see their birch bark canoes coming around the river's bend.

I had brought my friend Judi Miller Morris to a spot that Priscilla and I had long cherished, believing Judi would be moved to capture the spell of the place in water colors. Judi, who like myself grew up in Allegan and learned to love the nearby State Forest, completed her painting at the remote firetower in Wyoming where she spends her summers. Repeopled with the site's prehistoric inhabitants, the painting forms the cover of this book, the second of my *Romance of Michigan's Past* series.

This, my tenth book about the heritage of the state I love, contains 14 chapters about some little known but fascinating episodes in Michigan's past.

Sit back and let me entertain you with some true stories calculated to appeal to all who feel a romantic attachment to these two great peninsulas. Relive the tragic era when soldiers herded Potawatomi families from their beloved Michigan domain to the treeless prairies beyond the Mississippi. Hear pioneer women relate in their own words ordeals experienced in little log cabins amid the solitude of the big trees. Gallop through shot and shell of Civil War battles with other Michigan belles who served as nurses, spies, and disguised as soldiers. Brave the big waves of Lake Superior as a howling blow from the north strikes Whitefish Point - the graveyard of the Great Lakes.

Stalk the state's first celery grower. Listen to the likes of whiskey-voiced preacher George Wills and a host of other 19th century tipplers who discovered a lucrative pulpit calling when they swapped the bottle for the Bible. Ride along with dedicated saddlebag doctors, fording streams on horseback to visit patients. "Get out and get under" with pioneer motorists. Hop a train to the Columbian Exposition to view the amazing displays Michigan folks put together. Meet kindly little Father Sifferath, forgotten missionary to the northern Michigan Ottawa, and Dr. Crippen, the cold blooded killer from Coldwater.

My special thanks go to Nazareth archivist Sister Marie Traverse, who helped me greatly with research on Father Sifferath, to Amy Collins for her flying fingers and computer wizardry, to Loren McKinstry for his fine photographic processing, to my wife and partner Priscilla for her inspiration, and to the many kind people who encouraged me to write another book about Michigan's colorful past. Good reading!

Larry B. Massie
Allegan Forest

Potawatomi Tears

Me-Te-A, a distinguished Potawatomi Chief of the early 19th century.

She was a Potawatomi princess, proud and passionate, sweet and untamed, like the fruit of the pawpaw or frost-nipped wild grapes. But now she was the hare before the hunter. Fawn-like eyes wild with fear, shiny black hair matted and tangled, buckskin leggings and tunic dirty and briar ripped, gasping for breath while making a whimpering animal noise, she could run no further. Still she crawled through a sumac thicket and wedged her body fetal tight in a hollow in the grass where a deer had slept before. Whatever happened now would be beyond her power to resist.

She heard the crashing of the underbrush as her pursuers closed in. Face pressed to the ground, she felt the thud of horse hooves. They grew closer and louder then suddenly he was over her—a blue-coated soldier mounted on a perspiring horse. "Damn squaw," he spat. Sliding down from the saddle he roughly bound her wrists and ankles, slung her over the horse with a grunt and headed back to where the rest of his company had assembled their forest captives. It was a long ragged line of march, braves walking, heads bowed in shame, a few chiefs mounted on ponies, women and children, the old, the sick and the wounded tumbled into wagons—those who had fought to get away with wrists still bound.

The year was 1840 and it had been decreed that Michigan was not big enough for the peaceful Potawatomi and the new white masters of the land. Like the Cherokee and other tribes the Potawatomi would be led on a trail of tears—and death.

The Potawatomi had not always been a vanquished people—prey to pogrom. Not so long before they had held sway over Michigan south of the Kalamazoo River Valley, northern Indiana, Illinois and eastern Wisconsin—theirs a vibrant, rich culture that had achieved harmony with nature. Allied with the Ottawa whose domain bordered to the north and

14

Lacrosse, a native American team sport, was played on the ice in winter and on land at other times.

the Chippewa of the Upper Peninsula as "the people of the three fires," they spoke dialects of the Algonquian linguistic stock, and shared similar traditions, life styles and general appearance. The three tribes lived in peace with one another, sometimes intermarrying and dwelling in mixed settlements. They also banded together to fight their traditional enemies, the Iroquois to the east and the Sioux to the west.

The Potawatomi practiced a semi-sedentary existence, inhabiting larger villages, invariably located on streams navigable by canoe, in the growing season and after harvesting their fields of corn, beans and squash, broke down into family bands for migration to winter hunting grounds. They lived in dome shaped wigwams—usually a simple framework of poles, fastened together and covered with sheets of bark or with woven mats for better ventilation in the summer. Some smoke from cooking fires escaped through a small opening at the top of the wigwam, but the interiors were notoriously smoky.

Within the wigwam woven mats laid on the ground served as seats or when spread on wooden platforms as beds. Theirs was a self-sufficient economy—they took what they needed from the fields, the forests and the water. The Potawatomi flaked flint implements, projectile points, drills, knives and scrapers; ground stone ax heads and celts; molded pottery of clay tempered with stone particle; fashioned big wooden mortars and pestles for pounding corn into meal; wove bags and mats; carved wooden bowls and ladles; constructed trunks of rawhide and mococks of birch bark; tanned animal skins and furs for clothing, often with intricate painted designs and embroidered with dyed porcupine quills and moose hair.

The Potawatomi held council while smoking tobacco pipes made of clay or stone, danced, sang and played games—athletic events such as lacrosse, races and archery contests, snowsnake in the winter—and gambling games, dice and bowl and the game of straws. They traveled by snowshoe and toboggan in winter and in the other seasons preferred to paddle birchbark canoes, the construction of which they like the Ottawa and Chippewa had perfected to an art form.

With bow and arrows, snares, and traps Potawatomi braves hunted deer, bear, beaver, squirrels, rabbits, wild turkey, pigeons and the other diverse wildlife that rendered prehistoric Michigan a virtual Garden of Eden. They netted, hooked and speared trout, whitefish, pike, suckers and other fish. Standing on the high sandy bluffs of the Kalamazoo they watched for gigantic sturgeon working their way upstream through the shallows to spawn then raced down the bluff to wrestle the prehistoric monsters to shore.

To the women fell the task of planting and harvesting the crops. Women also foraged for wild fruits, nuts, mushrooms, roots, berries, wild rice and medicinal herbs. The entire family participated in maple sugar making.

The Potawatomi maintained a close-knit family life. White observers recorded many example of deep affection between husband and wife. Adults doted on papooses, and children, given the run of the camp, rarely suffered corporal punishment. Instead, humiliation was used to correct inappropriate behavior. Males furnished leadership in most areas, but within the wigwam the woman was unequivocally in command. The Potawatomi traced their ancestry through numerous clans such as Sturgeon, Eagle, Crane and Bald Eagle. Marriage within one's clan was taboo. Kinship was reckoned via the male lineage but children had the benefit of many mothers and fathers, such as their biological parents' brothers

Spearing fish from a tippy birchbark canoe required skill and balance.

and sisters and brothers- and sisters-in-law.

The Potawatomi worshiped a Great Spirit and also recognized the lesser deities of fire, sun, sea, and the four directions. They believed that objects such as rocks, plants and animals possessed manitous or supernatural power and that a personal manitou, or guardian, could be acquired by fasting and dreaming. The human body, the Potawatomi believed, had but one spirit, which after death followed a great trail to the west over the Milky Way, where there was an Indian heaven. Family members placed the bodies of the dead in temporary graves, sometimes in trees or scaffolds. When the Feast of the Dead was held every three to seven years, the bones of the dead were conveyed to the site and buried in a large communal grave along with their choicest possessions, amid much ceremony.

Potawatomi life at the time of European contact seemed close to idyllic with one major exception—intertribal war. Archeological evidence places the Potawatomi in southern Michigan by the mid 1400s. They had, according to tribal legends, previously inhabited the region north of Lakes Huron and Superior. In the 1600s came the eruption of the great French and British rivalry over control of the continent's fur trade. The British allied themselves with the Iroquois Confederacy of western New York. Incited to expand their trapping grounds and armed with European weapons the Iroquois conducted foray after foray into Michigan, easily defeating the resident Potawatomi and other tribes still employing stone age technology. By 1650 the entire lower peninsula of Michigan had been depopulated. Those that survived the Iroquois attacks fled to the Lake Superior region and western Wisconsin. Throughout much of the 17th century Michigan was a no man's land without permanent villages.

Then the Potawatomi and other Algonquin tribes

joined the French and began counter-attacking the Iroquois invaders, repeatedly defeating them in great pitched battles whose names have been lost in the mists of time. The displaced tribes began returning to Michigan in the late 1600s and following the end of the Iroquois threat in the early 1700s, the people of the three fires had reestablished themselves as the dominant tribes in the region which would become Michigan.

Fierce Potawatomi warriors continued to back their French Allies during the French and Indian Wars, participating in the Battle of the Wilderness and other bloody frontier engagements. Following the defeat of the French in 1760 and their loss of Canada and other territory east of the Mississippi, the Potawatomi switched to the British side, fighting against the Americans during the Revolutionary War and the War of 1812.

While the French and British had been content to trade with the Potawatomi and leave them in possession of their land the ever westward moving American nation sought to extinguish Indian title to their homelands through treaties. While theoretically more laudable than simply claiming the land by right of conquest, treaty making in practice often involved unscrupulous tactics such as stupefying the signers with whiskey, outright bribery and the recognition of lesser chiefs in favor of more legitimate leaders not inclined to sign. Whether the Indian signers fully realized the significance of the treaties based on white man's law is also doubtful. The failure of the U. S. government to fully honor the terms of the treaties was another bone of contention.

Beginning with a treaty made in 1785, which reserved the military posts at Detroit and Michilimackinac for the sole use of the United States, the Potawatomi and other Michigan tribes found themselves divested of increasingly larger blocks of

The "Brothers of the Three Fires" were fierce fighters. Here Chippewa braves battle the Sacs and Foxes.

their domain. In 1807, Gen. William Hull, who would win infamy through his surrender of Detroit in 1812, negotiated a treaty at Detroit which ceded most of the southeastern lower peninsula to the U. S. Michigan Territorial Governor Lewis Cass supervised the signing of the Treaty of Saginaw in 1819 which swallowed up another multi-million acre tract to the north and west. Two years later at Chicago, Cass and Solomon Sibly negotiated a treaty which cost the Potawatomi all their Michigan land south of the Grand River, with the exception of several small reservations. The 1833 Treaty of Chicago stripped the Potawatomi even of those reservations and in addition traded some five million acres in Indiana and Illinois for an equally sized tract on the treeless prairie of Kansas. The terms of the 1833 Chicago treaty allowed the Potawatomi three years to prepare for a gradual relocation to their newly alloted land west of the Mississippi. Additional treaties in 1838 and 1842 extinguished the rights of the Ottawas and Chippewas to all of their remaining domain in Michigan.

Removal of aboriginal Americans from their ancestral land to other less desirable locations had first been articulated as a policy by Thomas Jefferson in 1803. The idea received little attention, however, until after the War of 1812, which saw many Michigan Indians fighting on the British side. Andrew Jackson, a renowned frontier Indian fighter, used Indian removal as a presidential campaign issue in 1828. Two years after his election, Congress passed the Indian Removal Act. The official rationale for removal was to isolate the Indians from the debauchery and demoralizing influence of white traders and their whiskey so that they had a chance to acclimate to civilization. In reality, settlers, speculators, and town site developers lusted after their land. Jackson himself put it succinctly enough: "What good man would prefer a country covered with forests and ranged by a few thousand savages to our extensive republic, studded with cities, towns and prosperous farms..."

In the late 1820s and early 1830s immigrants from New York and New England launched a land rush for "Michigania" of epic proportion. The first waves of immigrants staked out the lush lands of the southern two tiers of Michigan counties, the heart of the Potawatomi domain. By then the Potawatomi legal holding had been reduced to the Nottawayseppe Reservation near present day Nottawa in St. Joseph County, a 64,000 acre tract near Athens, Calhoun County, a smaller reservation near of Niles and several other sites owned by individual Indians. Naturally, the Potawatomi continued to roam the forests and prairies of southern Michigan in pursuit of game and to camp in their traditional locations. Unfortunately, most of the fertile fields where they had long grown crops were coveted by the pioneers.

The pioneers did not seem to mind the presence of the Indians when they first began carving farmsteads out of the wilderness. Potawatomi muscle came in handy during barn raisings as did the haunches of venison and mococks of maple sugar the Indians swapped for next to nothing. But when the log cabins had been nicely chinked and the first harvests safely stored for winter use, the appearance of a hungry Indian family was quite another matter. Crisfield Johnson, author of the *History of Branch County* published in 1879, wrote what was undoubtedly a majority view:

...the vagrant begging habits of the Indians, those earliest of Michigan tramps, were unquestionably disagreeable to the enterprising and industrious pioneers of Branch County. When the noble red man, brawny and stalwart, but ready to starve to death rather than to do labor, sought food and

Sugar-making was dear to the hearts of the Potawatomi. This steel engraving and several of the others in this chapter are from Henry Schoolcraft's monumental six volume history of Indians.

shelter for himself, his wife, and his papoose, it was contrary to the custom of the emigrant from New England or New York to refuse such a trifle, but it roused his contemptuous anger to look upon a man so indolent and shiftless. All were anxious that the Indians should go.

The Potawatomi, on the other hand, were not at all anxious to leave their native land for the bleak western prairie, devoid of Michigan's forests and many streams and lakes. They knew what their alloted new land was like—delegations of Indians had traveled west to look it over and they had reported back. There would be no fish to catch, little game they were familiar with and no maple stands for sugar making. What's more, their traditional enemy, the Sioux, lived in close proximity. Jesse Turner, a Kalamazoo pioneer, remembered that "They would get dreadfully mad and their eyes would snap when anything was said about their going west."

Baw Beese, a good natured old Potawatomi chief whose village was near the present site of Hillsdale wept bitterly when pioneers told him that removal to the west was inevitable. "Sioux kill me; Sioux kill us all," he sobbed, "Sioux bad Indians, tomahawk squaw, scalp papoose; ugh!"

Nor was he the only chief to show such emotion in the face of forced removal to the west. Leopold Pokagon, a major chief who lived in southern Berrien County, "cried like a child" as he reluctantly signed the 1833 Chicago Treaty. But "the great white father in Washington" was not moved by weeping Potawatomi, and a torrent of tears would soon flow.

Although removal of the Potawatomi from Illinois and Indiana began as early as 1833, officials did not attempt it in Michigan until four years later. In the fall of 1837, a band of Potawatomi from the Niles area was mingled with a group from Illinois and pushed west.

Traditional Potawatomi travel on land included the use of travois.

Their hazardous journey, which required wading in Missouri for a mile through waist high floods, claimed the lives of one out of ten of the approximately 500 Potawatomi involved.

News of that terrible trek soon spread to the remaining Potawatomi and many began fleeing to the domain of their brother tribes in northern Michigan and to Canada where the British government welcomed with open arms its old allies to whom it felt an obligation to protect. In September 1838, Gen. John Tipton rounded up 859 Potawatomi, predominantly from northern Indiana but also approximately 150 from Michigan. Tipton captured many of the Potawatomi, including chiefs Menominee, Black Wolf and Peepehawah, by calling them in for a council and then surrounding the site with troops. At the point of soldiers' bayonets, the march west began on September 4. Six "rebellious chiefs" were carted west in a traveling cage.

Father Benjamin Marie Petit, a French priest who followed his Indian parishioners on their "trail of death" wrote a series of letters describing his experiences. Petit caught up with the line of march near Danville, Illinois, on September 16. He wrote the Rev. Simon Bruté, first bishop of Vincennes of what he witnessed there:

Soon afterward I saw my poor Christians, under a burning noonday sun, amidst clouds of dust, marching in a line, surrounded by soldiers who were hurrying their steps. Next came the baggage wagons, in which numerous invalids, children, and women too weak to walk, were crammed. They encamped half a mile from town, and in a short while I went among them.

I found the camp just as you saw it, Monseigneur, at Logansport—a scene of desolation, with sick and dying people on all sides. Nearly all the children, weakened by the heat, had fallen into a state of complete languor and depression. I baptized several who were newly born—happy Christians who with their first step passed from earthly exile to the heavenly sojourn.

The Potawatomi prison procession reached Indian Territory after one month of cruel march. The official journal of the expedition listed 43 Indian deaths en route. However, Petit did not think more than 650 Potawatomi arrived, although some managed to escape along the way. Other sources indicate that one out of five of the 859 Indians that started the trek died.

Following the 1838 Tipton trek which left fewer than 150 Potawatomi remaining in Indiana, the Michigan Potawatomi began migrating in large numbers to Canada. The best estimates indicate that nearly 1,500 Potawatomi reached Canada and stayed there, settling on Chippewa and Ottawa reservations stretching from Garden River near Sault Ste. Marie, Ontario, to Walpole Island on Lake St. Clair. A thousand or more Potawatomi also succeeded in remaining in Michigan by taking refuge with the Ottawa and Chippewa in the north. Still other bands eluded authorities by retreating to nearly impenetrable swamps in southern Michigan.

In 1840, urged on by the complaints of pioneers who wanted the Potawatomi off the land which they now felt was only theirs, Governor William Woodbridge applied to the federal authorities to remove all remaining Potawatomi from Michigan. Accordingly, in June 1840, Gen. Hugh Brady, a tough old veteran of Gen. Anthony Wayne's campaigns against the Indians in the 1790s and of the War of 1812, set out from Detroit for Marshall with force of 300 dragoons to begin the round-up. That summer the troops scoured the countryside for Indians, hired local pioneers familiar with the terrain to track them, decoyed Potawatomi into the open with promises of presents, and hog-tied and tossed over saddles and into wagons those who continued to resist.

David Lucas, pioneer from Bellevue in southern Eaton County and a friend of the Potawatomi recalled that:

> The Indians soon learned the troops were after them. A council meeting was held just west of the Bellevue settlement. They were mounted on the backs of their ponies all towards a common center. They were in deep, anxious consultation around their wisest heads. Soon they scattered like a flock of blackbirds. One company fled north, far into the forest. They had with them a sick squaw, which impeded their travel. They were overtaken and sought refuge in a dense swamp, which was surrounded by the cavalry, and after two or three days' siege, they were brought out of their hiding place and taken to Marshall, the place of rendezvous for those collected in this part of the state.

Brady's troops surprised old Baw Beese and his family while at a dance and marched them back to their village to gather up their possessions. Some of the local pioneers were sympathetic to the Indians' plight and gathered to bid them a melancholy farewell. Anson Van Buren, a Calhoun County pioneer, remembered handing out melons to each of the Indians as they sadly trudged by his farmstead. He recalled the old chief's pathetic farewell to those he thought were his friends: "Baw Beese endeavored to retain his customary calmness and self-possession, but nevertheless betrayed considerable emotion. As he took my father's hand his eyes filled with tears and he seemed to choke. 'Maybe go, maybe fight,' was all the expression he gave to his thought, and turning went his way."

Frederick M. Holloway, who had immigrated to Jonesville, Hillsdale County, that year, never forgot the mournful cortege of Baw Beese's band as it passed through that village:

> At the head of the column rode the aged chieftain in an open buggy, drawn by an Indian pony, alone, with his gun standing between his knees. A single infantry soldier, with musket on shoulder, preceded the buggy, while another marched on each flank. The chief had ceased to complain, but his countenance was dejected to the last degree as he drove in mournful silence away from the land of his forefathers.
>
> His wife, a woman of sixty, followed next, mounted on a pony, a single soldier being considered sufficient for her guard. After her came Baw Bee, a sub-chief, and half-brother of Baw Beese, with about a dozen more middle-aged and youngerly Indians and squaws, some on ponies and some on foot, and some of the squaws with papooses on their backs. These were probably the children and grandchildren of Baw Beese, and a special escort of a half a dozen soldiers was assigned to them.
>
> After these came the main body of the band, in groups of five, ten, or twenty each, stretching along for half a mile or more. A few were on ponies but most of them on foot; stalwart warriors, with rifles on their shoulders, but with mournful faces; women, still more dejected, with their blankets drawn over their heads; boys and girls, careless of the future, and full of mischievous tricks; and slung on their mothers' backs, the black-haired, bright-eyed, brown-faced papooses, the cutest-looking creatures in the world, gazing with infant wonder on the curious scene. On each side

of the road marched the soldiers, scattered along, a considerable distance apart, as if guarding a wagon-train.

The Indians were acquainted with almost every one , and as they recognized one and another of those who had been their friends, they called to them by name:

"Good-by, good-by."

"Good-by, good-by," responded the whites; and thus with friendly salutations the last of the *Pottawattamies* left for ever the home of their ancestors.

Kalamazoo pioneers remembered a similar scene as the Potawatomi who had been gathered there passed in a funeral-like procession through that community. The Kalamazoo contingent was made up of Indians herded from the north and west under the supervision of Col. Thomas Edwards, federal land office agent, and Henry Mower Rice, a government surveyor who would later make his mark as a Minnesota politician. For several days the captives camped in a field north of the present Amtrack Railroad Station and then began their march beyond the "Father of Waters." Guarded by a detachment of U. S. troops, the solemn file of Potawatomi trudged through the settlement, braves, heads held high stoically masking their emotions, sad faced women carrying papooses on their backs, ragged little children scampering about, too young to comprehend the true meaning of this adventure. Their ponies were piled high with copper pots, blankets and furs, ceremonial bundles, packets of seed corn—all their earthly possessions. Some of the elderly jolted along astride ponies, the feeble and sick were dragged in travois. As they passed the home of Judge Epaphroditus Ransom on South Burdick Street, a friend of the Indian and in whose hands some had placed their last ditch legal appeal to be allowed to

31

Judge Flavius Littlejohn of Allegan included this fanciful illustration of
Leopold Pokagon in his *Legends of Michigan*...published in 1875.

remain in Michigan, the Potawatomi braves "all doffed their ornamental head-gear, and elevated their right hands in token of a last good-bye."

Ransom apparently could do nothing to prevent the removal of the Kalamazoo Potawatomi. But he did assist a band of Berrien County Indians in thwarting the government round-up. When Chief Leopold Pokagon had learned of Brady's campaign, he had hastened to Detroit to plead his case with Ransom, an associate judge of the Michigan Supreme Court. Pokagon, a brilliant leader of approximately 250 Potawatomi, had planned his strategy well. He and his people had earlier embraced the Catholic faith, whose priests in opposition to many protestant missionaries including Isaac McCoy of the Carey Mission at Niles did not favor removal. They had also attended the Catholic missions established near Niles, learning the white man's language, farming techniques and other skills. Most significantly, Pokagon's band had wisely applied some of its treaty and annuity payments toward the purchase of land at the federal land office in Kalamazoo. By 1838 Pokagon had registered in his name a tract of 874 acres on Silver Creek, near present day Dowagiac. Abandoning their reservation near Niles, Pokagon's people moved to their Silver Creek holdings where they constructed log dwellings and a chapel and began farming the land.

Ransom concurred with Pokagon's contention that his band had secured a legal right to remain on their land. He wrote a legal opinion stating that Pokagon's band was under the jurisdiction of the state of Michigan like any other Christian, tax-paying, land owners, and if the federal troops attempted to forcibly evict the Indians from their property he would issue a writ of *habeas corpus* and have them returned to their homes. When Brady and his troops advanced on the Silver Creek settlement on August 17, 1840,

Pokagon presented the general with the legal opinion signed by Ransom. Brady scribbled out a "pass" that exempted Pokagon's band from removal, and returned to the chase elsewhere.

Not so fortunate were a band of non-Catholic Potawatomi who resided in the Athens, Calhoun County, vicinity. Lucius Buell Holcomb, a local trader and trusted friend of the Indians, accompanied them on their trail of tears and later wrote a heart-wrenching account of the inhumane treatment by the government Indian agents in charge of the migration. The agents had guaranteed the Indians that they would be taken by land the entire distance, together with their ponies and dogs. But at Peru, Illinois, they were driven aboard a boat at bayonet point and that was the last time they saw their animals as well as the copper kettles, guns and other personal belongings lashed to them. Conveyed down the Illinois River to the Mississippi and then up the Arkansas to their alloted reservation in Kansas Territory, they arrived in that inhospitable land at the onset of winter in a miserable impoverished condition.

En route, some like Chief John Moguago escaped. When Holcomb and some of the other Potawatomi journeyed back to Athens the following spring the first person they encountered was Moguago. While other Potawatomi also managed to sneak back to Michigan after removal most accepted their bitter pill of a new life in the treeless plains. As the 1840s wore on, the government forgot its Indian Removal Policy and most of Michigan's Ottawa and Chippewa were spared the trail of tears. But out of 400,000 Indians, only 18,000 remained east of the Mississippi after the removal tragedy.

Nor were the Potawatomi allowed to live unmolested in their new home. In 1848 all the Potawatomi in the west were herded together at St. Marys on the northern bank of the Kansas River, approximately 140 miles northwest of their original reservation in Linn County, Kansas. They remained there until the Civil War, when threatened by Confederate guerrillas and by the Sioux, they scattered to the north and south. Eventually some of the Potawatomi were granted other reservations in the new Indian Territory which ultimately became the state of Oklahoma. In 1937, the Department of the Interior counted 2,667 Potawatomi on the Oklahoma reservation and another 1,013 on the Kansas reservation . The Department of the Interior located only 142 Potawatomi remaining in Michigan that year.

The authors of many 19th century histories of Michigan counties marked the 1840 removal of the Potawatomi as the end of the pioneer era. George Torrey, who wrote a history of Kalamazoo County in 1869, echoed a common refrain: "Whatever may be said as to the justice of this act, there is no doubt but that removal was devoutly wished by the whites."

To other more sensitive pioneers, "after removal of the Indians the woods seemed lonely." James W. Hickok, an early Eaton County settler, lamented, "They had not been gone six months before we wished them all back. They helped us hunt and keep track of our cattle. If we lost an animal and described it to an Indian, he was sure to bring information where it could be found. When we had visitors, the Indians would furnish us with turkey or venison."

A year or two after removal, Baw Beese died in Kansas, "a broken-hearted man."

Pioneers in Petticoats

A matron remembers life on the Michigan frontier a half-century before.

G ripping the ornate walnut podium with her work-worn hands, Marion Withey gazed out over the crowd of gray-haired pioneers gathered in Lansing for their annual society meeting. Spotting familiar faces here and there and reassured that she was among friends, she began in a soft quavering voice, to tell of her childhood on the Michigan frontier a half century before.

"In the spring of 1833, my father Myron Hinsdill, came from Hinesburgh, Vermont, to Richland, then called Gull Prairie."

Withey had been but a little girl then, one of four daughters packed in the Conestoga wagon with all the other family possessions and jolted over Michigan's notoriously miserable roads to a new life among the park-like oak openings of Kalamazoo County. She told of hardships and suffering and the chilling sound of wolf howls while huddled in a primitive log shanty with a roof that leaked like a sieve. But even as she did, she paused to chuckle over a childhood recollection still vivid after all those years:

Mother had prepared the bread ready to bake in a tin oven before the out door fire, and gone to bed to have the regular ague shake, which came daily at the appointed time, leaving an older sister and myself to keep up the fire and watch the bread. Child-like, we were soon busy at play, and were only aroused to a sense of duty by seeing two great hogs walk off with poor mother's bread.

Laughter rippled over the crowd of pioneers. They knew well similar domestic tragedies suffered far from society's solace. Few of them had escaped bouts with the chills and fever of malaria, or the ague as they called it then. And they had learned that a sense of humor proved second only to stubbornness for

37

survival on the Michigan frontier.

Undoubtedly many another Michigan pioneer woman, like Withey, developed the talent to laugh in the midst of adversity. Unfortunately, relatively few recorded their experiences for posterity. Due in part to that fact and perhaps also because men tended to write the histories, textbook accounts of the settlement of Michigan acknowledge but rarely elaborate on women's role in carving a great state out of wilderness peninsulas.

Careful sleuthing among the dusty tomes, however, can leaven the traditional male oriented chronicles with feminine perspectives of pioneer life related in the actual words of the participants. And those stories are well worth the telling.

Anne Powell wrote one of the earliest descriptions by a woman of life in Michigan. An unmarried sister of William Dummer Powell, a chief justice of Upper Canada stationed at Detroit from 1789-1791, she accompanied her brother there in 1789. The territory now encompassed by Michigan had been awarded to the young nation as a result of the outcome of the Revolutionary War. But Great Britain refused to abandon the posts at Detroit and Mackinac Island. Powell's journal of her experiences at Detroit appeared in a biography of her brother published in 1924. She provides a rare view of high society on the first Michigan frontier:

As soon as our vessel anchored several gentlemen came on board; they had agreed upon a House for us , till my Brother could meet with one that would suit him. So we found ourselves at home immediately. We were several weeks at the Fort which gave us an opportunity of making a little acquaintance with the inhabitants. The ladies visited us in full dress tho' the weather was boiling hot. What do you think of walking about when the thermometer is above 90? It was as high as 96 the morning we were returning our visits. Mrs. P. and I spent the chief part of our time in our chamber with no other covering than a slip and under petticoat. We found all the people extremely civil and obliging. In point of society we could not expect much; it depends altogether on the Military, an agreeable Regiment makes the place gay. The 65th which we found there on our arrival was a Corps that would improve almost any society. The loss of it has made the place extremely flat and sets the present Regiment in a disadvantageous light, which it cannot bear. While we staid in the Fort several parties were made for us, one very agreeable one by the 65th, to an Island a little way up the River (Belle Isle). Our party was divided into five boats, one held the music: in each of the others were two ladies and as many gentlemen as it could hold.

Our party at the Island proved very pleasant, which those kind of parties seldom do; the day was fine, the company cheerful and the Band delightful. We walk'd some time in a shady part of the Island then were led to a Bower where the Table was spread for dinner. Everything here is on a grand scale; do not suppose we dined in a little English arbour; this was made of Forest Trees; they grew in a circle and it was closed by filling up the spaces with small trees and bushes which being fresh cut you could not see where they were put together and the Bower was the whole height of the Trees, tho' closed quite to the top. The Band was placed without and play'd while we were at dinner. We were hurried home in the evening by the appearance of a Thunder Storm. It was the most beautiful sight I ever remember to have see. The clouds were collected about the setting sun and the forked lightning was darting in a thousand directions from it. You can form no idea from anything you have seen of what the lightning is in this country; these lakes, I believe are the nurseries of Thunder-storms, what you see are only stragglers that lose their strength before they reach you. I had the pleasure of being on the water in one and getting very completely wet. My clothes were so heavy when I got out of the boat, I could scarcely walk. We were a very large company going up on what is commonly called a party of pleasure. Most of the ladies were wet as myself. We could get no dry clothes so were obliged to get our own dried as well as we could. A pretty set of fogires we were when we met to dance, which, on those occasions, is customary before dinner. I had resolved against it for the day was very warm, the party large and the room small. I was prevail'd upon to alter my mind by their assuring me that exercise would prevent my feeling any ill effects from my wetting, and I found it so.

The British finally relinquished Detroit to the Americans in 1796 and that brought a sudden end to such high society there. Other aspects of life would not remain so idyllic either due to the continued threat of hostility by the Indian tribes in Michigan who had fought on the side of the British during the Revolutionary War. The situation came to head with the outbreak of the War of 1812.

Eighty-three year old Mrs. Nancy Howard of Port Huron penned her valuable recollections for the *Detroit Free Press* in 1889. Born in Fairfield, Pennsylvania, in 1806, she moved with her family to Detroit in 1812. Her father Jonathan Hubbard was a fur trader there:

We had lived in Detroit but a few months when

Immigrant life on the go.

father rented a farm at Grosse Pointe, where we moved in time to put in fall crops. While we were a long distance from English neighbors, there being only one other family between the point and Detroit, yet we felt quite contented as our prospects were quite bright, until father was taken ill and died in the middle of the winter. His remains were laid to rest on the banks of Lake St. Clair. No language can express the anguish of that hour. A wife without a husband and eight children without a father and so far from friends and home surely we could say we were strangers and in a strange land. After retiring from the grave and the darkness had settled down so black and gloomy, we sat about the old fashioned fireplace in sadness and anguish. I could not bear it long, and going to my eldest brother I crowded in between his knees looked him in the face, and said: "Edward, will you be a father to me?" The silence broke into tears, but in a moment he replied: "Yes, my dear sister, so far as I can."

Very soon after our severe trial the dreadful news came of war being declared with England, and the dear brother in whom we had placed so much reliance, volunteered for six months. He provided his own horse and was appointed to mounted sentinel duty between Detroit and Grosse Pointe, to guard the river shore.

Mother remained on the farm to secure what crops were possible. It was while we were there alone that we were one day surprised by the blood-thirsty savages. I was in the yard, and, looking up onto the lake, I espied a canoe load of Indians coming near shore. A squaw was coming up the road and when she was opposite the house she beckoned and at that moment they sprang on shore and ran up to the fence, leaped over it with the agility of deer and ran up to the house. We saw the whole proceeding from a window, and fully expected that our time had come. My eldest sister sprang to the door and her first impulse was to lock it and did so, but again turned the key and opening the door as they came up, in French she asked them to come in and get warm, as it was a cold day. They shouted to her and she turned and walked into the kitchen where mother and the children were sitting around the fireplace. The Indians followed and surrounded the family. As they stood there in their war paint, with their tomahawks and scalping knives in readiness, they did present a most hideous spectacle. They discussed the situation between themselves to considerable length, not being certain that the family were English after what my sister had said to them in French. In a few minutes, however, my sister took up the youngest child and walked out of the back door, and mother and the rest of the family followed, going across the fields to the nearest French neighbor.

The Indians then most thoroughly plundered the house of nearly everything save my sister's clothing, which they knew by the size. The dishes they took down to the beach and broke them into pieces. They then went up the lake shore several miles and related the circumstances, saying that if we were not French they would come back that night and kill us, but they were assured that we were French. Notwithstanding this they seemed determined to kill us, and word was sent us to leave the house. This we did for several nights but came back during the day.

Thanks in part to that ruse, the Hubbard family survived the Indian terror. Fear of Indian massacre, however, motivated Gen. William Hull to surrender Detroit without firing a shot on August 16, 1812.

Another little girl, who would become Mrs. Eliza Scott Schettler, also described an encounter with Indian culture. The daughter of a merchant stationed on Mackinac Island, she never forgot an incident that took place in 1810:

I remember one day while my brother Mich.and I were skipping stones on the beach our attention was attracted by the sound of hard blows and distressed cries from a dog. On running to the spot, we found an Indian paddling a fox-colored dog to death. Mich. was a dauntless little fellow, and at once seized hold of the paddle, while I threw my self over the dog to protect him. After some exclamations of astonishment from the Indians, the squaw said "eat, boil," pointing to the kettle of boiling water, thus adding to our horror. At our protest she said, "Pork, me give you dog," so I staid to cover the dog, while the little man ran as fast as possible to the store, and told the clerk to give him, quick, a big piece of pork. Holding it tightly in his arms, he came back and made the exchange to the three parties interested and we led the little fox-colored dog home. Mother, with a rather dubious expression on her face, consented to our keeping the dog, but said that we had better not go near the camp any more. We named the dog Prince and as each month passed, we concluded that he was well named, as he became a faithful, intelligent little fellow.

The Straits of Mackinac region was also the scene of the recollections of Elizabeth Therese Baird. Born in 1810 of a French father and Indian mother, she was married on Mackinac Island at the age of 14. Some 60 years later she described a sugar making party on nearby Bois Blanc Island:

Frequently, each season near the close of sugar-making, parties of ladies and gentlemen would come over from Mackinac, bent on a merry time, which they never failed to secure.

One time, a party of five ladies and five gentlemen were invited to the camp. Each lady brought a frying-pan in which to cook and turn *les crepes* or pancakes, which was to be the special feature and fun of the occasion. All due preparation was made for using the frying-pan. We were notified that no girl was fitted to be married until she could turn a *crepe*. Naturally, all were desirous to try their skill in that direction, whether matrimonially inclined or not.

The gentlemen of the party tried their hand at it, as well as the ladies. It may not be amiss here to explain what to turn the *crepe* meant; when the cake was cooked on one side, it was dexterously tossed n the air and expected to land, the other side up, back in the pan. Never did I see objects miss so widely the mark aimed at. It seemed indeed that the *crepes* were influenced by the glee of the party; they turned and flew everywhere, but where wanted. Many fell into the fire, as if the turner had so intended.

Some went to the ground, and one even found its way to the platform over the head of a turner. One gentleman (Henry S. Baird) came up to Mrs. John Dousman, and holding out his nice fur cap, said, Now turn your cake, and I will catch it.. Mrs. Dousman was an adept at turning, and before the challenger had time to withdraw his cap, with a toss she deftly turned the cake and landed it fairly into the cap. You may imagine the sport all this afforded. In due time, a nice dinner was prepared. We had partridges roasted on sticks before the fire; rabbit and stuffed squirrel, cooked french fashion; and finally had as many *crepes*, with syrup, as we

All eyes were on mother during baking day.

desired. Every one departed with a bark of wax and sugar cakes.

With the danger of Indian warfare eliminated following the end of the War of 1812, settlers again began braving life in Michigan. As an elderly matron, Mary Anne Brevoort Bristol, like Baird, also relished culinary memories and other aspects of the domestic side of life in Detroit of the 1820s:

The way the bread was made and baked was like this: There was a large box, something like a chest with a cover, which had four legs for supporters, like a table; the dough was mixed at night; this chest was called in French, *"une huche;"* in the morning the dough was kneaded and moulded, placed on boards to rise.

A log house was about two hundred feet or more from the residence, in which there was an oven built of poles and clay; the oven heated with just so much wood split very fine and burned to coals, which were burned out; it was then mopped with a mop and a pail of cold water, which left the oven warm and clean; the bread was carried there on the boards; it was placed on wooden paddles or shovels, and put in the oven, which had a sheet iron door and a wooden one over, that closed tight—what sport it was to carry it there; when baked, what a beautiful sight to look at, eighteen or twenty loaves of bread, all yellow as gold.

We had wooden churns and wooden water buckets, made something like kegs of the present day; we had also a wooden yoke made to fit the shoulders and neck, with a piece of rope on each end, and a hook made of iron to hitch to the bucket, and every drop of water which we used was carried from the river, no matter how far the house stood from it.

Saving ice was an unknown thing in those days. The water was brought from the channel of the river, put in large jugs, and buried in the ground to keep it cool.

When the young men, members of the family, wished for fresh meat, all they had to do was to step back of the house at the edge of the woods where the Michigan Central railroad now passes, and kill a deer, put a rope around his neck and draw it home.

In one of the rooms a large spike was driven, upon which they hung the deer to dress it; the spike is still in the beam. They thought nothing of dressing from four to five per week

They also set traps to catch wolves, which were numerous, by digging a hole in the ground, about eight feet deep, and large enough to catch as many as possible at one time; they would place a door on top, and put fresh meat in the hole. The minute a wolf stepped on the door, it would tip, let him in and close up; another would come, he was served in the same way. In that way, they caught great number; each head brought a bounty; it was great sport, and money making business at the same time.

Chimneys were built the same as the ovens, with poles, straw, and clay, which when dry were solid and very hard.

All the washing was done in the river, by driving two stakes and placing a piece across to hold the end of a plank or log, eight or ten feet long, the other end resting on the shore. Upon the end on the water, whoever washed, would sit on a stool, dip the piece in the water, rub on the soap, and pound with a short handled paddle called a "battois."

As the decade of the 1820s wore on, more and

more brave souls ventured into the interior of southern Michigan. Sarah Bryan, who with her husband and five children pioneered the wilderness near present day Ypsilanti in 1823, gave birth to the first white child born in Washtenaw County, appropriately named Alpha Washtenaw Bryan. Decades later she told her gripping saga of almost superhuman strength and courage:

It was amusing that first fall and winter to hear the corn mills in operation every morning before daylight. There were but two in the settlement, made by burning a hole in the top of a sound oak stump, large enough to hold a peck or more. After scraping the coal clean from the stump, one end of a stick, some six feet long and eight inches in diameter, was rounded, and it was suspended from a spring-pole so that the rounded end would clear the stump when hanging loosely. A hole was bored through this pestle and a stick driven through projecting on each side for handles, and the mill was finished. One man would pound a peck of dry corn in half an hour so that half of it would pass through a sieve for bread; the coarser part being either ground again or boiled for hominy. Very little bread of any other kind was used in the settlement for the first two years. But as regards my own experience, the autumn of 1824 was the most trying. Thus far we had encountered few more inconveniences than we anticipated in the wilderness, and I was prepared for them, prepared to bear all without a murmur. In October Mr. Bryan accepted an offer to finish a building at Maumee City (Toledo) and shipped his tools at Detroit, where he had been doing an eight month job. He came home and stayed a few days to provide some wood, and told me if he was likely to be more than three weeks absent, he would return at the end of that time and put up more provisions, as our small stock would be then exhausted. No person had then attempted to penetrate the forest from our place to Monroe, but rather than go round by Brownstown, (later renamed Flat Rock) he determined to take the risk of finding his way through the woods alone. My heart sank within me to think of what would be my fate and that of my six children, if any evil should befall him alone in the forest; I however summoned my fortitude and resolved not to be faint-hearted.

The three weeks passed; a good supply of potatoes was nearly all the provisions we had left, and I began to look with great anxiety for my husband. A felon on my right hand deprived me entirely of the use of it for more than three weeks. With the pain, fatigue, and want of sleep I was ready to despair, but for my children's sake I kept up my resolution; still no tidings came from Mr. Bryan, and my fears for his safety became more and more painful. Two months passed, and brought cold December for me and my little one, but brought no news from him whose duty it was to provide for us. My sufferings became extreme. I tried to get some one to go in search of him, and ascertain at least if he ever got through the woods alive, but I had no money even to bear expenses, and all told me they 'guessed' he was safe and would soon return. How myself and babes were to live meanwhile we knew not. We had eaten nothing but potatoes for several weeks; the neighbors were nearly as destitute and had nothing to lend, even if I could have borrowed when I could not expect to pay again. For a temporary change in diet from potatoes alone, I ventured to borrow a few ears of corn, promising to pay if Mr. Bryan ever returned; this I shelled and boiled to jelly, which we relished very much while it lasted.

It was now the 23rd of December; I had been all day trying to induce some one to go to Maumee for tidings, and had succeeded in obtaining a promise from a young man that he would go in two or three days if I would get a horse. Alas! horses were as scarce as bread, and I knew it would be impossible to procure one. I returned home and stood in our log cabin door, thinking what to do next, when my husband rode up, and put an end to my fears. He had written several letters, which were delayed in Detroit, and never reached me. Finding wages high, and the roads very bad, he had concluded to remain, supposing I was well provided for. Our sufferings for five or six years after this were even greater, if possible, than before, but it would take a volume to describe them.

Another Washtenaw County pioneer woman, who emigrated with her husband from western New York in 1824 to settle near Dexter, echoed a similar story of suffering and survival. Harriet Noble's recollections were published in 1852 in one of the earliest compilations to chronicle the feminine role in the frontier, Elizabeth Ellet's *Pioneer Women of the West:*

We cooked our meals in the open air, there being no fire in the house but a small box-stove. The fall winds were not very favorable to such business; we would frequently find our clothes on fire, but fortunately we did not often get burned. When one meal was over, however, we dreaded preparing the next. We lived in this way until our husbands got a log house raised and the roof on; this took them about six weeks, at the end of which time we went into it, without door, floor, chimney, or anything but logs and roof.

51

Ravenous wolf packs were but one of the perils of life on the Michigan frontier.

I helped to raise the rafters and put on the roof, but it was the last of November before our roof was completed. We were obliged to wait for the mill to run in order to get boards for making it. The doorway I had no means of closing except by hanging up a blanket, and frequently when I would raise it to step out, there would be two or three of our dusky neighbors peeping in to see what was there. They would always give me such a start, I could not suppress a scream, to which they would reply with "Ugh!" and a hearty laugh. They knew I was afraid, and liked to torment me. Sometimes they would throng the house and stay two or three hours. If I was alone they would help themselves to what they liked. The only way, was to threaten that I would tell (Lewis) Cass; he was governor of the territory, and they stood in great fear of him. At last we got a door. The next thing wanted was a chimney; winter was close at hand and the stone was not drawn. I said to my husband, "I think I can drive the oxen and draw the stones, while you dig them from the ground and load them." He thought I could not, but consented to let me try. He loaded them on a kind of sled; I drove to the house, rolled them off, and drove back for another load. I succeeded so well that we got enough in this way to build our chimney. My husband and myself were four days building it. I suppose most of my lady friends would think a woman quite out of "her legitimate sphere" in turning mason, but I was not at all particular what kind of labor I performed so we were only comfortable and provided with the necessaries of life.

Many times I had been obliged to take my children, put on their cloaks, and sit on the south side of the house in the sun to keep them warm; any thing was preferable to smoke. When we had a chimney and floor, and a door to close up our little log cabin, I have often thought it the most comfortable little place that could possibly be built in so new a country; and but for the want of provisions of almost every kind, we should have enjoyed it much. The roads had been so bad all that fall that we waited until this time, and I think it was December when my husband went to Detroit for supplies. Fifteen days were consumed in going and coming. We had been without flour for three weeks or more, and it was hard to manage with young children thus. After being without bread three or four days, my little boy, two years old, looked me int he face and said, "Ma, why don't you make bread; don't you like it? I do." His innocent complaint brought forth the first tears I had shed in Michigan on account of any privations I had to suffer, and they were about the last. I am not of a desponding disposition, nor often low-spirited, and having left New York to make Michigan my home, I had no idea of going back or being very unhappy. Yet the want of society, of church privileges, and in fact almost every thing that makes life desirable, would often make me sad in spite of all effort to the contrary. I had no ladies' society for one year after coming to Dexter, except that of sister Noble and a Mrs. Taylor, and was more lonely than either of them, my family being so small.

Many another Michigan heroine of the home counted lack of society among the worst of the hardships she had to bear. The solitude of a homestead in a little clearing surrounded by the nearly impenetrable forest actually drove some women insane. Yet, despite loneliness and hardship, life on the Michigan frontier offered families a chance to better themselves through hard work.

Following the completion of the Erie Canal in 1825, which provided a relatively faster and easier journey to Michigan, the trickle of settlers from western New York and New England became a torrent. Then came a land rush for "Michigania" of epic proportions. Travel across Michigan territory, however, improved but little.

When Richard Dye emigrated from Herkemer, N.Y., to the Ionia vicinity in 1837 and began carving a homestead out of the wilderness, his wife was left to follow with her two small children. She took the Erie Canal to Buffalo and then boarded a steamer for Detroit, where her husband awaited with a wagon for the overland travail:

> We next set about preparing for our journey to our future home. Enough provisions were secured before leaving Detroit to last two years. We loaded one barrel of flour on our wagon and shipped the rest of our provisions around the lakes, so that they would come to us by the way of Grand Rapids. The provisions that we loaded on our wagon we thought would last us to the end of our journey. Thus the day was passed in preparation and nothing else occurred worthy of recollection. The days flew away as we traveled through the almost unbroken country, seeing nobody save our little band of pilgrims, and hearing nothing save the howling of wild animals, in the dark primeval forest, where the echo would resound through the hollow quietude of nature and the world seemed hushed with the solemnity of death. At night we camped by the side of some stream or stayed whenever we could, at some farmhouse, resuming our journey as early in the morning as possible.
>
> The first village at which we stopped was Pontiac, where we remained over night, at the house of an

old friend, and spent a few of the most joyous hours of my life. We proceeded in the morning on our journey through the unbroken wilderness, meeting meanwhile, some bands of Indians, with which we did some trading. We finally reached those terrible swamps which lay in the valleys of this country, the largest of which was about two miles across, and the only way we succeeded in crossing was, by having one of the men to take a long pole and, standing on the end of the wagon tongue, probe the water on either side and also in front, so as to ascertain the depth and thereby to prevent us from being drowned or otherwise injured. That night we stopped at the house of a Dr. Laing, taking lodging only, for which in the morning we paid the usual fee of five dollars (a week's wages at that time).

It was some time before we took shelter in another house and, meanwhile, our provisions becoming very scarce, we had to be as economical as possible, living chiefly on bread made of Indian corn. At last the crisis came; overcome by hunger, tired and exhausted, wet, cold, and disheartened, we found ourselves at the very door of starvation. After traveling all day we were not able to obtain shelter or relief till very late in the evening, when we came to a log hut, where we partook very heartily of the hospitality of those living there and rested for the night. In the morning we resumed our way, very much refreshed. Our journey throughout was marked with hardship, toil, suffering, cold, hunger and almost starvation and to add to our troubles there was an abundance of flies, gnats and mosquitoes, which were so numerous that the sky was completely darkened. The only way by which we were able to free ourselves from the mosquitoes was by cutting branches of small trees and using them as brushes.

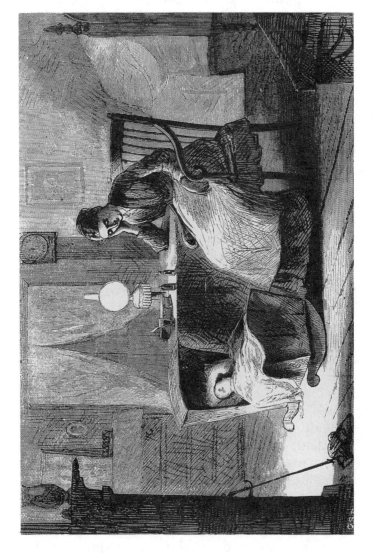

Frontier motherhood featured frequent nocturnal vigils over sick babies.

It would require too much time for me to describe in minute detail the scenes through which our journey led us, but they are nevertheless, as fresh in my memory as the events of yesterday or today.

Caroline Kirkland, one of the most highly educated American women of her time and used to the sophisticated society of New York salons, found herself transplanted to the raw Michigan frontier in 1837. Her satirical descriptions of the hardships and indignities she encountered comprise some of the most readable accounts of pioneer life. In 1837, she traveled to Pinckney, 60 miles northwest of Detroit, with her husband, a myopic professor turned land speculator, and small children. She captured the vicissitudes of that journey and life in the rugged frontier community in *A New Home: Who'll Follow*, published in New York in 1839.

The roads near Detroit were inexpressibly bad. Many were the chances against our toppling load's preserving its equilibrium. To our inexperience the risks seemed nothing less than tremendous—but the driver so often   reiterated, "that a'n't nothin'," in reply to our despairing exclamations, and, what was better, so constantly proved his words by passing the most frightful inequalities in safety, that we soon became more confident, and ventured to think of something else besides the ruts and mud-holes.
Our stopping-places after the first day were of the ordinary new country class—the very coarsest accommodations by night and by day, and all at the dearest rate. When everybody is buying land and scarce any body cultivating it, one must not expect to find living either good or cheap: but, I confess, I was surprised at the dearth of comforts

which we observed every where. Neither milk, eggs, nor vegetables were to be had, and those who could not live on hard salt ham, stewed dried apples, and bread raised with "salt risin," would necessarily run some risk of starvation.

One word as to this and similar modes of making bread, so much practiced throughout this country. It is my opinion that the sin of bewitching snow-white flour by means of either of those abominations "salt risin'," "milk emptin's," "bran 'east," or any of their odious compounds ought to classed with the turning of grain into whiskey, and both made indictable offenses. To those who know of no other means of producing the requisite sponginess in bread than the wholesome hop-yeast of the brewer, I may be allowed to explain the mode to which I have alluded with such hearty reprobation. Here follows the recipe:

To make milk emptin's. Take quantum suf. of good sweet milk- add a teaspoon full of salt, and some water, and set the mixture in warm place till it ferments, then mix your bread with it; and if you are lucky enough to catch it just in the right moment before the fermentation reaches the putrescent stage, you may make tolerably good rolls, but if you are five minutes too late, you will have to open your doors and windows while your bread is baking.

"Salt risin" is made with water slightly salted and fermented like the other and becomes putrid rather sooner; and "bran 'east" is on the same plan. The consequences of letting these mixtures stand too long will become known to those whom it may concern, when they shall travel through the remoter parts of Michigan; So I shall not dwell upon them here—but I offer my counsel to such of my friends as may be removing westward, to bring with them some form of portable yeast (the old fashioned dried cakes which mothers and aunts can furnish, are as good as any)—and also full instructions for perpetuating the same; and to plant hops as soon as they get a corner to plant them in.

Caroline Kirkland never really did fit into the mold of pioneer life. And when copies of her book containing criticisms of uncouth frontier manners and thinly veiled characterizations of actual Pinckney residents circulated back to that community, the author soon found herself *persona non grata*. Eventually the Kirklands moved back to New York, where, sadly, her near-sighted husband drowned when he accidentally walked off a wharf. She pursued her literary career, specializing in stories about her brief, albeit memorable, life on the Michigan frontier.

Few of the other women who braved the Michigan frontier had the opportunity, like Kirkland, to pull up stakes and return to civilization back east. Their lot was to remain on their isolated homesteads, scrimp and scrape and hope for better times for their children. Harriet Noble concluded her testimony about pioneer life in Washtenaw County with a poignant statement that must have been echoed by many another heroic Michigan pioneer woman:

When I look back upon my life, and see the ups and downs, the hardships and privations I have been called upon to endure, I feel no wish to be young again. I was in the prime of life when I came to Michigan—only twenty-one, and my husband was thirty-three. Neither of us knew the reality of hardship. Could we have known what it was to be pioneers in a new country, we should never have had the courage to come; but I am satisfied that with all the disadvantages of raising a family in a new country, there is consolation in knowing that our children are prepared to brave the ills of life, I believe, far better than they would have been had we never left New York.

Churning butter and the other tasks demanded of log cabin life rarely allowed a spare moment for frontier wives.

Whitefish Point: Grave-yard of the Great Lakes

The lighthouse tower at Whitefish Point was constructed in 1861.

Thirty five miles northwest of the Sault Locks, jutting like the beak of a gigantic gull, Whitefish Point guards the gate to the grandest body of fresh water on the face of the globe. The sanctuary of Whitefish Bay lies to the lee of the sandy Peninsula. But beyond the horizon, north and west, stretches a vast sweet-water sea. The native Ojibwa worshipped that deep dark lake as Gitche Gumee, a moody deity prone to veil its features in mist or suddenly lash its tranquil beauty into a terrifying tempest of wind and waves. Its howling gales and fog-shrouded sorcery have littered its bottom with broken ships and broken men. The Whitefish Point region, where more vessels have gone down than in any other part of the lake has well earned its title—graveyard of Lake Superior.

Sunny blue days at Whitefish Point bring tourists who glance up from their agate combing to marvel at mirages strung along the horizon, imaginary islands that come and go. And when the fog signal bellows, some have peered long into the swirling mist to glimpse the ghostly outlines of birch bark bateaux, full-rigged schooners and whaleback ore carriers. The sound of the surf throbs with the pulse of the past—the faint echoes of merry voyageur songs and the crack of canvas billowing before the mast.

And some have sensed the spirits that people the Point—Chippewa chiefs and couriers de bois, black-robed Jesuit priests and blue coated soldiers, fur traders and fisherman, ship captains and shanty boys, Cornish, Finnish and Irish immigrants bound for a new life in the Copper Country; light house keepers and life saver surfmen.

A glance at the map soon shows why the Whitefish Point region became the graveyard of the lakes. Roaring across Lake Superior for 160 miles, north winds have reached more than 90 miles per hour at the Point, rearing up monstrous waves over 30 feet in height. Eighty miles of treacherous coast with harbors of refuge only at Grand Marais and Marquette lies to the west of the Point. Whitefish Bay offers sanctuary but it also functions as a great funnel through which all of Lake Superior's upbound and downbound vessels must pass. The big Lake's notorious fogs and smoke from forest fires often compounded the chances for collision or running aground, especially in the days before the introduction of radio beacons. Occasionally, complications such as engine problems and blunders by captains have sent other great vessels to the bottom.

Pierre Esprit Radisson and his brother-in-law Medart Chousant Dieur des Groseilliers became the first Europeans to record their impressions of Lake Superior following explorations there in 1658. Returning to New France with an immense fortune in furs, their success inspired many daring entrepreneurs to exploit fur trading opportunities in the Lake Superior region. Responding to the European lust for furs, beaver in particular, licensed traders, free lance couriers de bois, and the colorful work horses of the fur trade, voyageurs, pushed ever deeper into the wilderness. For a century and a half voyageurs paddled their great birch bark bateaux past Whitefish Point, hugging the coast out of respect for Lake Superior's sudden fury.

One of the earliest recorded shipping disasters to occur in the Great Lakes graveyard related to the fur trade. As a result of a feud between the North West Company and the rival Hudson Bay Company, in 1816 Lord Selkirk of the latter company led an attack on Fort Williams on the Canadian North Shore. He arrested some key Northwest Company employees and sent them east for trial in some large cargo canoes. Big waves capsized one of the canoes near Parisienne Island northeast of the Point on August 26, 1816. Eleven of the 24 persons aboard drowned.

Jesuit missionaries carrying the cross to the wilderness passed Whitefish Point in birchbark canoes.

Later that November one of the Northwest Company leaders sailed from the Sault for Fort William, armed with a court order, in the little fur trading schooner *Invincible*. Jean Baptiste Perrault, a Northwest Company voyageur, recorded what befell the vessel: "Toward the middle of the traverse of *la pointe aux poissons blancs* (Whitefish Point), a violent wind from the north west came up; the weather turned cold, which , in a moment, froze the sails and cables, so that they were powerless to manage the vessel." Driven ashore just south of Whitefish Point, the *Invincible* was smashed to pieces. Amazingly, all aboard survived the ordeal although they suffered great hardships making their way back to the Sault.

In 1821, the two British fur trading companies patched up their differences and joined forces. By then John Jacob Astor's American Fur Company had begun to make inroads in the Lake Superior fur trade. A military force under Michigan Territorial Governor Lewis Cass had conducted a 4,000 mile canoe expedition through Lake Superior the year before to assert American authority in the north country. Two years later Fort Brady would be established at Sault Ste. Marie. Henry Rowe Schoolcraft, a member of the Cass expedition who would be stationed as Indian agent at the Sault, penned a narrative of the journey in which he described Whitefish Point as "a barren peninsula of sand, stretching a considerable distance into the lake, with a few aspen trees, and rising in some places are naked hills of sand, which the wind is continually whirling into the air, and depositing in bands and ridges, like drifting snow."

In 1826, United States Indian Agent Thomas McKenney conducted another canoe voyage along the southern coast of Lake Superior. In company with 65 blue-coated infantrymen he was bound for Fond du Lac to negotiate a treaty between the warring Chippewa and Sioux tribes. After camping for the night in the vicinity of the mouth of the Shelldrake River, a few miles south of Whitefish Point, the expedition got an early start the following morning. McKenney described his impressions of the Point and his entry into the big lake in *Sketches of a Tour to the Lakes* published in 1827:

Atmosphere thick and damp. Run up the shore of Whitefish Point, which stretches far out into the lake. A barren sand point, with nothing on it but drift wood. Not even a pine tree can live upon it—and it is as level as it is lifeless. It derives its name from the fish of this lake, and on account of its being a fine place for taking them. From the Canada shore, nearly opposite, projects another point—the opening between them may be eight miles. On passing this opening, we are fairly out upon this great lake, whose vast sheet of water was seen when the fog subsided, as far as the eye could take it in. Hitherto, and when out in the lake, or bay rather, the shores of Canada could occasionally be seen; but now all to our right, and in front is one vast ocean of transparent water, over which air as pure as ether perpetually hovers in stillness, or blows in tempests. Variety is the character of this region. The elements appear to have nothing else to do but amuse themselves.

In the summer of 1832, Schoolcraft conducted another canoe voyage from Sault Ste Marie along the southern shore of Lake Superior and into present day Minnesota, ultimately accomplishing his goal of discovering the source of the Mississippi River at Lake Itasca. The commander of Schoolcraft's military escort, Lt. James Allen, recorded a detailed narrative of the journey which was published by the government in 1834. Allen commented on the recent beginnings of the first commercial exploitation of the Point's

Thomas L. McKenney, Indian agent, described Whitefish Point in 1826 as "a barren sand point with nothing on it but driftwood."

fabled fishing grounds:

> This point is remarkable and important as a fishery of whitefish—as affording more, and a better quality, of that excellent fish, than any other fishery of the southern shore of the lake yet explored. It has been long known as a point where this fish could be taken in gill nets at certain seasons of the year; but no use was made of it, more than is at present of several other fisheries of the lake, where a few Indians, or an individual trader, procure only what is necessary for their immediate subsistence. But within the last two years the enterprise of two gentlemen, Mr. (Samuel) Ashmun and Mr. (Ecstache) Roussin (Raussain), who had retired from the fur trade of the American Fur Company has developed many facts, in relation to this fishery tending to show its importance as a course of business and profitable trade.
> These gentlemen commenced the business of fishing at this place two years ago, without any particular knowledge or experience, with regard to the seasons, localities or the best means of taking the fish, and notwithstanding these disadvantages,have made it a source of considerable profit, and are encouraged to continue it more extensively.

The year 1835 witnessed the advent of something else which would develop into a vital aspect of the region's economy—tourism. That summer, Dr. Chandler Robbins Gilman and Maj. Murray Hoffman earned the distinction of becoming Lake Superior's first tourists. The pair journeyed from New York City on a "leisure trip" to view the Pictured Rocks near present day Munising, which they had read about in previous travel narratives.

Arriving at Mackinac Island via a steamship, there the tourists secured a 30 foot long bateaux, manned by four French Canadian voyageurs and an Indian guide. Five days later they landed at Whitefish Point where they found three log huts and four Indian lodges inhabited by fishermen. A dozen Indians and half-breeds greeted the tourists. Gilman, who had begun to miss his wife's companionship, noted in his two volume travel narrative published in 1836 that: "They were much better looking than any Indians we had hitherto seen, and one of the women, though no longer very young, was quite handsome; she was full Indian."

After spending the night with the fishermen and feasting on whitefish, the party shoved off early the next morning. Gilman, like many a later tourist rhapsodized the beauty of the lake:

It was a glorious sight. As the East began to glow with his first beams, the high bluffs on the Canada side, that had before seemed like blue clouds hanging on the verge of the horizon, assumed a purple hue; and then as the first direct rays from the risen sun darted athwart them their sides were broidered with the golden beams. Nature seemed to have put on her royal robes in joy and triumph that the storm had passed away.
Her smiling aspect spread cheerfulness over us all; and as we left the shore, I thought I had never heard our men sing so merrily; the music was evidently in accord with their feelings.

The American Fur Company had established the commercial fishing venture at Whitefish Point, described by Allen, Gilman and other writers, to bolster the rapidly declining fur trade. During the 1830s the operation proved successful. The company launched three schooners on Lake Superior to transport thousands of barrels of whitefish and trout each season and it constructed a new warehouse in Detroit to store those barrels. Ultimately, however, the fishing industry proved too successful. The market could not consume the number of fish caught and prices plummeted. That, coupled with the depression which swept the nation following the financial panic of 1837, brought the failure of the company's commercial fishing venture. The American Fur Company went bankrupt in 1842. Commercial fishing on Lake Superior would languish for over a decade.

But even as the fur and fishing industries fell by the wayside something even bigger loomed on Lake Superior's economic horizon—mineral wealth. For centuries rumors had circulated of the fabled masses of native copper to be found in the Upper Peninsula. However, the true extent of the mineral deposits remained a mystery. Douglass Houghton, Michigan's first state geologist, had learned of the presence of copper in the Keweenaw region while accompanying Schoolcraft on his 1832 journey to the source of the Mississippi River. In 1840 he mounted an expedition to explore and map the Keweenaw Peninsula.

Houghton and party left the Sault in a large Mackinac boat on June 1, 1840. Charles W. Penny, a young Detroit merchant who accompanied the expedition, kept a journal of his experiences. At Whitefish Point, Penny described seven or eight wigwams pitched in the sand. The geologists stopped there and brewed a cup of tea before continuing around the point. Then the voyageurs "put on their towing line and harnessed themselves into it, and we moved off in real canal style—the beach forming one of the best tow paths imaginable." The party progressed but a few miles before camping for the night. During the night a storm blew in preventing their traveling the next morning.

As they waited for the weather to improve, the

grandeur of storm-lashed Lake Superior moved Bela Hubbard, assistant geologist to the expedition, to pen a poetical description in his journal:

Far abroad the "white caps" are seen enlivening the dark blue surface, but as the gale sweeps the waters of the broad expanse over onto the southern shore the whole force of the immensely deep lake seems compressed into the narrow depth now allowed it and rises into mad breakers which roll huge volumes, tumbling impetuously towards the beach. The line of gathering waves is seen far out joining into one, huge, long uplifted wave, which presses majestically on, lifting higher and higher its threatening crest, as if rushing over a precipice, then comes thundering down in a tremendous sheet of foam and flying spray, tearing up the sands and with a roar that seem to shake the coast. Broken in its majestic march it then spreads into lines of lesser breakers and sweeps, foaming, high up the beach. Between these successive ridges of breakers, the water seems absolutely drawn away, recoiling backwards and thus adding height and violence to the gathering mass.

As the waves sweep up the beach and recede again to await the next succeeding lash, at one place the beach will be left bare for the distance of many feet, while in the next instant with a hissing rush and foam it is thrown with gradually lessening force, to your very feet.

The sublimity of this scene is increased by the continued roar which accompanies it. This is not alone that of the dash of water, however loud. But distinct from the rush of waves and the howling blast of the wind is a deep under-toned bass—the lowest conceivable note in the incessant music of nature; distinct, prolonged, filling up every pause

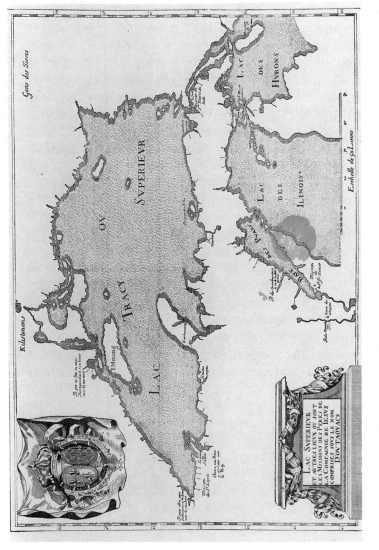

This map appearing in the *Jesuit Relations* of 1672 pictured several imaginary islands in Lake Superior.

in the awful harmony.

Get-rich-quick adventurers eagerly read the published reports of Houghton's 1840 expedition which documented the existence of copper in the Keweenaw region and his subsequent efforts to promote the Upper Peninsula's mineral wealth. Unfortunately, Houghton's promising career ended in 1845 when he drowned in the icy waters near Eagle River, but not before he had launched a frenzied dash for red metal that rivaled the "49ers" later California gold rush. Government surveyor William Austin Burt also located massive lodes of iron ore in the Marquette vicinity in 1844.

As the Upper Peninsula's economy quickened through the presence of thousands of prospectors seeking to strike it rich, most of whom returned poorer but wiser men, and entrepreneurs established the first of the copper and iron mines, additional ships began plying the dangerous waters of Lake Superior.

In 1847, *New York Tribune* editor Horace Greeley paid a visit to the booming copper country. Appalled by the government's failure to fund maritime safety features, Greeley wrote a fiery article, citing, in particular, the urgent need for a lighthouse at Whitefish Point, already infamous for the many shipwrecks in its vicinity. "Every month's delay is virtual manslaughter," he wrote. Greeley's editorial blast may have spurred the federal government to move ahead with maritime improvements in Lake Superior. In any event, the shipping season of 1849 witnessed the first operation of a lighthouse at the Point. Constructed of stone hauled from an island off the north of the Tahquamenon River, the lighthouse stood 65 feet tall and was 25 feet in diameter at the base. The lighthouse's original whale oil lamp would be replaced a decade later by a much brighter Fresnel lens consisting of a bee hive shaped series of prisms which magnified the light into a single bright beam.

The completion of the Sault Canal in 1855, under the supervision of Charles T. Harvey, opened up a new era for Lake Superior shipping. No longer would ships and cargo need to be laboriously and expensively portaged around the St. Marys Rapids. With the elimination of the shipping bottleneck at the Sault more and larger vessels, heavily laden with copper and iron ore, began passing Whitefish Point.

While the Whitefish Lighthouse undoubtedly helped make maritime travel safer, the Great Lakes graveyard continued to claim its victims. On June 6, 1859, the 350 ton propeller *Indiana*, loaded with iron ore from Marquette, sprung a bad leak several miles west of the Point. Fortunately, the 21 people aboard managed to make it to shore in a yawl before the *Indiana* plunged 118 feet to the bottom.

Two years later, the original stone lighthouse which proved too weak to withstand the buffeting of severe storms at the Point was replaced by a 78 foot tall "iron pile" tower resting on masonry piers. More than 130 years later that "skeletal frame" continues to support its cast iron watch room and lantern.

Still the Point continued to take its toll. The 167-foot schooner *Grey Eagle* ran aground at Whitefish Point in July 1869. The savage surf soon pounded it to pieces. An October storm in 1871 blew another schooner, the *Plover*, ashore near the Point, and she also was a total loss. All aboard the two wrecks lived to tell of their experiences.

Not so fortunate were the crews of the *Saturn* and *Jupiter*, big schooner barges filled with iron ore. A fierce blow from the north struck as the vessels neared Vermilion Point, ten miles to the west of Whitefish Point, on November 27, 1872. The force of the gale snapped their tow lines and the barges were blown aground just west of the Point. The savage surf and bitterly cold wind spelled doom for all of the 15 persons aboard the barges.

An edition of John Disturnell's Great Lakes tour guide published two years after the tragedy contained a chilling warning concerning the perils of travel west of Whitefish Point:

> In all the navigation on Lake Superior, there is none more dreaded by the mariner than that from Whitefish Point to Grand Island, and this is especially the case late in the season, when the fall storms make navigation the most hazardous, and the heaviest and most valuable freights are on transit. This coast is exposed to every wind that blows from the Lake, the sweep being of its full width and length, and there is not at present a single place where a landing can be made, or a lake steamer or vessel run for safety, in the whole distance of 80 odd miles. The entire coast is made up either of the towering cliffs at the western end, the bleak hills of sand at the Sauble Banks, coming down to the water's edge and offering no landing, except for a small boat in pleasant weather, or the dull low beach beyond—stretching away for nearly 50 miles farther with one single insignificant creek—the Two Heart River—that a Mackinac boat can possibly enter if in smooth water, excepting always the harbor of Grand Marais—to which there is no entrance for large vessels. This beach is strewed with wrecks from the Pictured Rocks to Whitefish Point.

Nor were storms and freezing surf the only dangers to be reckoned with in the graveyard of the Great Lakes. As the century wore on and ship traffic increased each year the chances of collision at the Whitefish Bay funnel increased. On August 26, 1875, Francis Dugot, captain of the 181 foot propeller *Comet,* accidentally swung his vessel broadside in front of the sidewheeler *Manitoba*. The bow of the *Manitoba* sliced a gaping gash in the *Comet's* wooden hull and she soon plunged 240 feet to the bottom of Whitefish Bay, taking 11 of the 21 aboard with her as well as her cargo of 70 tons of Montana silver ore en route to the Philadelphia Mint.

The year 1876 witnessed the creation of the U. S. Life Saving Service in the Great Lakes. All of the original life saving stations on Lake Superior were established along the deadly stretch between Whitefish Point and Grand Marais. By May 15, 1877, life saving stations had been established at Vermilion Point, Crisp Point, the mouth of the Two Hearted River and Deer Park. As no roads existed to those isolated sites, barges floated in material from the Sault to construct headquarters buildings, two-story boathouses and cookhouse. Each shipping season, from April until December, surfmen stationed at the stations scanned the lake from watch towers, patrolled the beaches in shifts at night, maintained their life saving boats and other equipment and practiced drills such as firing lines in a little brass cannon to establish a breeches buoy to transport passengers off wrecked vessels.

But when the notorious Lake Superior fogs shrouded the waters there was little the life-savers could do to avert the frequent collisions that occurred in the heavily traveled shipping lanes. On July 27, 1884, the steel passenger steamer *Alberta* suddenly shot out of the fog, slamming her bow deep into the wooden steam barge *John M. Osborn*. The barge was nearly sliced in two by the force of the collision. Fortunately, the vessels hung together long enough for all but four of those aboard the *Osborn* to leap onto the *Alberta* before she plunged to the bottom near Whitefish Point.

And the terrible gales that swept in from the north continued to take their toll. When the 138-foot

U. S. Life Saving Service sailors brave the breakers in a self righting lifeboat in 1880.

schooner barge *Eureka* broke her tow line during a savage northern storm on October 20, 1886, she went down off Vermilion Point. Despite the search efforts of the Life Saving Service surfmen the bodies of the five persons aboard were never seen again.

The *Niagara,*another schooner barge loaded with iron ore, met a similar fate when a gale roared in from the northwest on September 7 of the following year. Her tow line snapped and the giant waves soon capsized the 205 foot long vessel near Vermilion Point. The captain and his crew of nine attempted to pull for shore in their lifeboat, but the raging surf rolled it over and all drowned.

On June 19, 1889, the steel freighter *North Star* rammed a similar vessel, the *Sheffield* during a dense fog. Nearly severed in half, the *Sheffield* slid below the waves off Whitefish Point. Fog also brought about the collision of the wooden steamer *Samuel Mather* and the *Brazil,* a steel freighter on November 22, 1891. The *Mather* plunged 185 feet to the bottom of Whitefish Bay. The following September the bow of the wooden steamer *Nipigon* splintered the hull of another wooden steamer, the *Vienna,* for no apparent reason in clear weather. Within an hour the *Vienna* had also settled to the bottom of Whitefish Bay. Miraculously all aboard the vessels involved in those three collisions survived their ordeals.

An accident on July 29, 1901, however, would claim the lives of the captain and a sailor of the *Sagamore,* one of the odd-looking whaleback barges invented by Alexander McDougall. While anchored in the downbound channel waiting for a heavy fog to lift, the *Sagamore* was rammed by the 300 foot steel steamer *Northern Queen.* With a jagged gash in her steel hull, the *Sagamore* soon sunk to the bottom near Iroquois Point.

Two other vessels went to the bottom of Vermilion Point on October 2 of that same year, as a result of bad luck. The wooden steamer *Drake* had been towing the schooner barge *Michigan* in heavy seas when the *Michigan* signaled that it was taking on water and would soon sink. The *Drake* circled back alongside and while in the process of transferring the *Michigan's* crew a huge wave smashed their two hulls together. The force of the collision sent the *Drake's* smoke stack crashing to the deck. All aboard the *Michigan* managed to scramble aboard the *Drake*, but without its stack the boiler fire lost its draft and went out. Powerless she was battered about by the heavy seas until she took on too much water and settled below the waves. Two passing steamers rescued everyone except the unfortunate cook, who was forgotten in the confusion.

The twentieth century would bring progressively more sophisticated navigational equipment and improvements to the lighthouse at Whitefish Point. But even as stronger and bigger ships passed the Point many tragedies would occur. The captain and a crew member went to the bottom of the Great Lakes graveyard with the 192 foot wooden steamer *William F. Sauber* in 1903. Five sailors drowned when the *Alexander Nimich*, a 298-foot wooden steamer, was battered to pieces in a fierce gale near Vermilion Point. When the *Isaac M. Scott* plowed into the *John B. Cowle*, a 420-foot steel ore boat, in 1909, 14 of the crew died. The entire 16 man crew of the 186 foot lumber hooker *Myron* perished in the icy water when a raging November blow smashed the vessel to kindling in 1919. A year later and five miles southeast of the Point, another freighter rammed the 429-foot *Superior City*. Twenty-nine sailors died when her boilers blew and the ship plummeted 265 feet to the bottom.

Several other vessels met their fates in the Whitefish Point vicinity during the 1920s. Then came a long period when it appeared that the curse of the shipwreck coast had dissipated. Freighters grew larger and there were fewer of them. Sophisticated technology seemed to have tamed Lake Superior. Captains felt their huge ships invincible—some lost their respect for the big lake—they developed hubris.

Then on November 10, 1975, a killer storm roared down from the north. Winds in excess of 90 miles per hour heaved up monster waves, 30 feet and more in height. Caught in that tempest, the 727-foot ore boat *Edmund Fitzgerald* lost its race for the shelter of Whitefish Point. The "pride of the American flag" lay in three jagged sections 530 feet below the surface of Lake Superior, 17 miles northwest of Whitefish Point. The big lake never surrendered the bodies of the 29 men aboard.

When the irresistible force worshipped by the Chippewa as Gitche Gumee will litter the graveyard of the Great Lakes with yet another victim no one can tell—that it will no one but a fool can doubt.

Healers on Horseback

Pioneer doctors often forded streams on horseback.

K alamazoo County's first physician, Dr. Nathan Thomas, slumped forward in the saddle, bone tired. It was October, 1834, and he had been up all night ministering to patients at their homes in Schoolcraft. Returning to his office he found a message scratched on the slate attached to the front door—a sick woman in Paw Paw needed him. Thomas slung the saddlebags containing all his instruments and entire pharmacy over the saddle, wearily climbed back on his steed and set out on the 18 mile ride through the thinly settled wilderness.

The horse's rhythmic pace had rocked the exhausted medic asleep in the saddle, the horse took a wrong turn on the trail, and Thomas woke at dawn, not in Paw Paw, but at another settlement several miles out of the way. When he finally reached Paw Paw and attended to the sick woman, he rode back to Schoolcraft and spent the rest of the day with his other patients.

Thomas' medical career was typical of the saddlebag doctors who served Michigan's pioneers. Like itinerant judges and preachers, they made rounds over wide territories. Thomas' practice extended over a sparsely settled area 30 miles in diameter. Two months after he began his practice in 1830 he succumbed to an attack of fever. After attempting to treat himself unsuccessfully for ten days, he sent for the only other doctor in western Michigan, located 25 miles away in White Pigeon Prairie. Thomas soon recovered and for the next seven years he never left his practice for more than a day at a time.

Although Thomas credited his long hours in the saddle as the exercise that kept him healthy, by 1853 the hard regime had physically worn him out. Following a severe attack of rheumatism he quit his medical practice.

The harsh lives of pioneer doctors, lack of sleep and long nighttime rides broke the health of many.

One of Allegan County's first physicians, Dr. Osman D. Goodrich , set up practice in Allegan in 1836. The little village on the Kalamazoo River was surrounded by wilderness without a single house between it and Lake Michigan. To further complicate matters Goodrich's wife and child took sick soon after his arrival.

By 1845, the privations of pioneer doctoring had so impaired his own health that he quit his practice and moved to Ohio. There he became a disciple of a new school of medical thought called homeopathy.

Homeopathics dispensed small doses of drugs that produced on a healthy person effects similar to that of the disease. As strange as this theory seems, it sometimes proved better than the traditional massive doses of powerful drugs then administered by regular physicians. In 1855 Goodrich returned to Allegan to become the first homeopathic physician in the county.

Saddlebag physicians were a diverse lot, yet typically they embodied certain common qualities. Though many were medically self-trained or educated via the apprenticeship system they tended to possess a greater than average general education. They were often free-thinkers, somewhat eccentric and, because of the long hours spent alone in the saddle, individualistic. While practicing a traditionally selfless profession, many were also active in social reform movements. Most were charitable to the point of injuring their own livelihood and, quite naturally, beloved by the community.

Few pioneer doctors better typified the ideal than Dr. Uriah Upjohn of Richland. A native of Shaftesbury, England, Upjohn emigrated with his older brother, William, to New York in 1828. He began "reading medicine" under an established doctor at East Albany. Several years of apprenticeship and attendance at the "College of Physicians and Surgeons" in New York City earned the 36-year-old Upjohn his medical degree in 1834.

After a year's practice in Brighton, New York, Upjohn and brother, William, who had also picked up a medical degree, set out to seek their fortunes in Michigan Territory. They made their way to Kalamazoo County via Lake Erie by steamer, then overland on foot through the oak openings. A quarter section of government land near Richland, available at $1.25 an acre, caught their eye. They soon built a log cabin and hung out their shingle. Dr. William Upjohn later moved to Hastings where his practice of over forty years was interrupted only with service during the Civil War as surgeon to Gen. George Armstrong Custer's 7th Michigan Cavalry.

Dr. Uriah Upjohn stayed on at Richland. For more than twenty years, until the roads had been improved enough for buggy travel, he rode a medical circuit among the desolate pioneer cabins scattered over five counties. His service to the sick often went above and beyond contemporary expectations.

One day, while visiting patients at a remote settlement, he learned of a sick family off in the wilderness. After a roundabout ride through the woods he arrived at a log cabin to find an entire family of eight prostrate with fever. "Water," they croaked, as he entered the door. He filled a pitcher at a nearby lake, dispensed medicine, chopped wood, built a fire, made them comfortable, and left with the soothing words that he would soon return. He then rode another three or four miles out of the way to find a neighbor to look after the sick family through the night.

Upjohn long remembered another experience that happened during the summer of 1838, known as the "sickly season." He had been on the road for two or three days attending to the ill at nearly every cabin. As he wearily rode and led his horse toward home a galloping rider overtook him. A sick woman at a

NATHAN M. THOMAS, M.D.

The likeness of Dr. Nathan Thomas of Schoolcraft appeared in the 1880 *History of Kalamazoo County.*

cabin north of Yankee Springs urgently needed help. Upjohn hesitated, it would be a 26 mile ride. "was she very sick?" he asked. "Yes, very," replied the messenger, "and very poor; you may never get your pay." Upjohn scrawled a note to his wife for medicine to be delivered by the man and made his way back, arriving at the woman's pitiful log hut at three o'clock the next morning. Not only was there no food for the doctor, but the log barn held nothing but straw for his horse.

Despite his demanding labors Upjohn rarely asked poor families for payment. In 1880, he reckoned that during his 45 years of practice he gave half of his services to the destitute. Yet, during that time, he somehow managed to raise his own family of 12 children. Eleven lived to adulthood, a high percentage for those times. Five chose their father's profession and graduated from the Medical Department of the University of Michigan. Mary and Amelia became the first women graduates in pharmacy, and Helen, Henry U. and William E. received regular medical degrees.

Beginning in 1885, William E. would parlay a little manufacturing operation that specialized in his invention, the "friable pill," into what would become a Fortune 500 corporation and Kalamazoo's largest employer, the Upjohn Company.

In the pioneer days Dr. Uriah Upjohn dispensed large quantities of quinine for a wide range of illnesses including pneumonia. Quinine, however, was particularly suited for one prevalent pioneer disease, the ague, now recognized as malaria. Few pioneers escaped the alternating fever and chills of the ague. While the disease was rarely fatal, it made life miserable. During the illness a fit of "shakes" would incapacitate the victim and occur so regularly that pioneers adjusted their schedule for well days and ague days. Pioneers noticed that the ague occurred most commonly near swampy areas and developed a number of theories to account for this including the inhalation of vapors arising from rotting vegetation. They never suspected that the true cause lay in the bites of the hordes of mosquitoes that bred in the swamps. When the low lands were drained for agricultural purposes malaria gradually disappeared.

Other common pioneer illnesses were more deadly. Unhygienic living conditions brought typhoid or "brain fever" epidemics. Scarlet fever, diphtheria, measles, mumps, small pox and other contagious diseases appeared frequently. Many children, in particular, died from the croup. Pneumonia or "lung fever", often prevalent in winter, occurred as a milder form during the days of drafty cabins and open fireplaces than later when tight houses and stoves came into general use. Cancer, heart ailments and other diseases generally affecting older persons attracted little attention because most pioneers did not live long enough to develop them.

Cholera periodically ravaged the Michigan countryside, and its high fatality rate rendered it a particularly dreaded disease. Several epidemics struck Detroit in the early 1830s. Out-state pioneers set up road blocks to prevent infected persons from traveling westward. In 1850 an outbreak in Kalamazoo occurred coincidentally with the arrival of Paulus Den Blyker's party of Dutch immigrants. With no hospital yet in existence, terrified citizens herded the Hollanders into a run down pest house, and several more died from the effects of exposure.

Many pioneers doctored themselves with folk remedies that had changed little since the days of Shakespeare. A cold or a sore throat called for a piece of fat meat with pepper tied around the neck, grease from the Christmas goose, mustard and onion poultices, bloodroot and cherry bark, or rock candy and whiskey. Sheep dung tea, popularly known as "nanny tea" would hasten the breaking out of measles. A poultice of cow dung held in place by a stocking turned wrong side out was a sure way to avoid diphtheria, or at least ward off potential carriers of the disease and everyone else!

During the 1830s popular journals promoted a new panacea—the tomato. Eaten daily, cooked or raw, the tomato prevented bilious attacks, cured dyspepsia and diarrhea, and rendered one less susceptible to cholera. Later, Kalamazoo patent medicine entrepreneurs discovered celery to have similar curative properties, particularly for nervous afflictions.

The rigorous system of the pioneer doctors sometimes "killed quick but cured slow." A standard technique was letting out the bad blood via copious bleeding. Doctors inadvertently poisoned patients with massive doses of calomel, or chloride of mercury, that brought on intense salivation. Frequently, these procedures did little more than further sap the patient's strength. Yet pioneer doctors also practiced techniques recommended by the best medical authorities and eagerly accepted new advances. Before Michigan became a state in 1837 territorial doctors were vaccinating pioneers against smallpox.

A variety of alternative schools of medical thought arose during the first half of the nineteenth century in opposition to the severe methodology of the regular physicians. When homeopathics prescribed minute doses of drugs that produced on a healthy system effects similar to the patient's complaint, allopathic doctors recommended drugs that did just the opposite, and eclectics let the patient, or next of kin, choose their own type of treatment. Although all these theories combined elements of quackery and were fought tooth and nail by the regulars, they at least helped steer the profession away from the traditional "shotgun doses" of powerful drugs.

Another avante garde medical movement that

Dr. Osman D. Goodrich was Allegan's first doctor on horseback.

became particularly popular on the Michigan frontier was known as the Thomsonian system. Samuel Thomson, a New Hampshire farmer, had adapted some ancient medical theories into a regimen based on vegetable or "botanic" remedies in conjunction with the vapor bath. Thomson patented his system and granted rights to practitioners on receipt of a fee. The Thomsonian system appealed to frontiersmen because they distrusted book learning and, to a certain extent, regular physicians, it seemed more democratic, and one could cheaply become a Thomsonian doctor. Despite the creation of county medical societies and licensing requirements in Michigan during the 1830s, for all practical purposes, anybody was a "doctor" who called himself one.

Whether candidates decided to become doctors because of altruism or a desire for prestige few expected the medical profession to prove lucrative. Doctors, like most other pioneers, scraped for a living. Dr. Nathan Thomas initially found his practice so poor that he could not even put aside enough money to purchase government land at $1.25 an acre. Another early Kalamazoo doctor reckoned his total yearly earnings after expenses as 12 1/2 cents. What little available money circulated on the frontier rarely went for doctor's services. Some hard-pressed doctors resorted to newspaper notices pleading for settlement of overdue accounts or actually published lists of debtors.

With specie scarce, physicians eagerly accepted other articles of barter including livestock. Sometimes they got the bad end of the bargain. When a new doctor set up practice in Charlotte he received a hog for professional services. It was a thin specimen and the doctor made a deal with a farmer to fatten it on corn and then butcher it for half of the product. The farmer fed it corn one night and promptly butchered it the next morning, telling the angry doctor that it was fat enough for his own use and, he thought, for the doctor's as well. Although cheated, the doctor gained such a reputation as a result of the widely circulated story that his patronage increased substantially.

Other doctors also got the last laugh when cheated on a barter. During the early 1860s Dr. Homer Hitchcock of Kalamazoo treated a young man for heart disease. The patient ran up a large bill and knowing Hitchcock was a horse fancier offered to supply a good horse in exchange. When Hitchcock received his equine fee he soon learned it was balky and no good, but the patient said the deal was final. The Civil War draft started soon after, and the same young man appeared before the local physical examiner—Hitchcock. He slapped him on the back and told him he was on his way to war. The reluctant recruit exclaimed, "Why, Dr. Hitchcock, you know you treated me for heart disease...don't you remember it?" "Yes," said the doctor, "but that was before you traded me the horse!"

Many pioneer doctors demonstrated generosity and kindheartedness that their patients never forgot. Dr. Salmon King, the first settler and first physician in Augusta, visited every settler's cabin in the region on medical or social calls. When criticized by his family for his poor earnings he replied that "the burden of illness was sufficiently hard to bear, without the addition of a heavy fee."

Similarly, during the 1820s, Dr. James B. Dunkin pioneered on Nottawa Prairie. Dunkin grew ample grain, but many of his neighbors were extremely poor. When a person sought grain, Dunkin asked, "Have you money to buy it with?" The man answered, "Yes, sir, I have the means to pay for what I need." "Then," said Dr. Dunkin, "I cannot let you have any, for you can get it elsewhere. I am going to keep what I have got for those what have no money to buy with."

A Civil War veteran from Otsego, Dr. Milton Chase, sadly remembered the necessity for combining a number of professions. After spending a long night in a log shanty with a woman in labor, the baby was born dead. He put in another half day building a crude casket, digging a grave, saying a prayer and comforting the bereaved mother.

Generous, kindhearted, hard working or merely eccentric, for whatever reason they were remembered, physicians filled important roles in the pioneer community. If their medical knowledge was primitive by modern standards, their presence brought hope and their cheering words fostered recovery. By the Civil War era, the pioneer period had ended in southern Michigan. Settlers had converted the wilderness into prime homesteads. Better roads made life easier as doctors traded the saddle for the buggy. But long hours, hard work and little financial reward remained the doctor's lot. It was a rare event when a practitioner could record, as did Dr. Edwin Stewart of Mendon on May 28, 1858, "Have seen nobody's tongue today."

Black Bags & Buggies

Heavy fur coats like that worn by Dr. Homer Hitchcock of Kalamazoo
were a necessity for horse and buggy travel.

The fever epidemic raged across Kalamazoo County's rural Alamo township. Dr. Paul Butler had been up for three nights visiting the isolated farm houses. His trusty horse knew the way home, so he laid the reins across the buggy's dashboard, curled up on the seat and drifted off to sleep. Suddenly he awoke with a start. The horse had stopped, the night was pitch black and the buggy trembled and swayed. Dr. Butler knew it was an earthquake. He clung desperately to the buggy as it pitched more violently and from underneath came rumbling, grinding and unearthly groans. When he peered over the side Butler realized what had happened. His weary horse had walked over a cow asleep in the road and Bossy, under the buggy, was trying to get up.

A half century had elapsed since saddlebag doctors first tended southwestern Michigan pioneers. The buggy had replaced horseback as the favored mode for making house calls. Plenty of other things had improved as well. Physicians no longer routinely mortified patients with blood letting and doses of poisonous mercury compounds. And while medical fakirs and patent medicine hucksters still bamboozled gullible sufferers, state and local medical academies better regulated the genuine profession.

The University of Michigan Medical School had gained a fine reputation since its inception in 1850, and by 1866 six full-time professors lectured to 550 students. Burgeoning enrollment, however, greatly increased demand for anatomical cadavers. Michigan law provided no legal means for their procurement, and as a result the University of Michigan Medical School periodically enlivened headlines with grave robbing scandals. Across the midwest, mourners guarded tombs to protect the deceased from professional "resurrectionists."

The final third of the nineteenth century saw the stethoscope, microscope and clinical thermometer come into general use. And, to the chagrin of many a sick youngster, doctors now employed hypodermic needles, huge and blunt by modern standards. Yet the general rule for cases of compound fracture remained amputation—the risk of infection was too great. Anesthesia was available in operating rooms, but country doctors seldom resorted to it. While physicians performed "kitchen surgery" or sewed up lacerations, patients drank whiskey, cursed, prayed or did all three.

A doctor's schedule, particularly in country practice, still divided itself into two components—getting to the patient and doing something at the bedside. Improved roads and more comfortable buggy seats made the first part easier. A good horse and buggy could average seven miles an hour in cold weather and good roads. On muddy roads, three miles an hour was considered good. Naturally, most sicknesses occurred in inclement weather and at night.

In winter, doctors replaced their buggies with sleighs and encountered a new set of difficulties. Kalamazoo medical historian, Dr. Rush McNair, recorded his sleighing adventures that began in 1887. He remembered dodging huge snow drifts on country roads by driving through the fields back and forth over old rail fences. Red flannel underwear, a thick overcoat with high fur-lined collar, a fur cap, a heavy buffalo robe, and soap-stone foot warmers were necessities for winter driving. But even such equipment failed when cutters overturned in snow banks, or the doctor had to flounder on foot through deep snow to reach a patient's house. Dr. Gerald Rigterink's father, a country practitioner, went so far as to clip his horses' coats every fall so they would run faster to keep warm.

Other stories about horse and buggy doctors reveal their emotional, human qualities. Dr. John

Dr. Elmore Sill made daily horse calls to patients in 1870.

Bosman of Kalamazoo trained his beloved horse and dog, Jimmie, who always followed beside the buggy, to kiss each other on command. When Jimmie died at the age of 13 his master wrote an eloquent eulogy in his honor. Dr. George King of Mattawan and veteran Kalamazoo physician, Dr. Gilbert Rose, spent a long night together at the bedside of a dying man. Returning home the following hot midsummer morning, they both dozed off in the buggy. A front wheel ran into a hole, pitched both doctors forward, and the axle broke, tumbling them under the horse's heels. King scrambled out and sat on a rock, but as soon as Rose caught his breath he began to vent his feelings. He cursed "the horse, the buggy, the road and even the dust and ruts, night work of doctors, the whole doctoring business, the day he was born and that he should be condemned to set the affairs of this lost vermin infested world aright." King laughed himself almost to exhaustion.

Despite the somewhat improved transportation and medical equipment, some things had scarcely changed since the pioneer era. Scientists were yet to comprehend the bacterial origin of contagious diseases, and many now tamed diseases annually killed hundreds throughout the region. Rows of tombstones in country cemeteries bear silent witness to diphtheria epidemics that wiped out entire families within days. Scarlet fever swept neighborhoods and killed or permanently deafened survivors. Many others slowly died of consumption, what contemporaries call tuberculosis.

Better medicines had become more widely available, but few doctors wrote prescriptions to be filled at apothecaries. Instead, they compounded and dispensed their own remedies. Some prescriptions might seem odd by today's standards. Civil War veteran, Dr. Foster Pratt, served on the U. S. Pension Examining Board in Kalamazoo during the 1880s.

When old and disabled veterans came before the board and asked Pratt what they should do for their weariness, weakness, shortness of breath or digestive distress, he invariably advised, "Take a drink of whiskey every day. I don't mean a sip—take a good big drink." Pratt was also somewhat eccentric in that he did not keep an office but saw patients at his home, their home, the lobby of the Burdick House or even on the street. A local wit quipped, "It costs $5 to shake hands with Dr. Pratt on the street."

Long working hours, hard drives and poor pay persisted well into the horse and buggy era. Kalamazoo's Dr. Herman Schaberg, for example, routinely arose in the middle of the night to visit patients and then raced back for a full day of office calls. Dr. William Bovie, a beloved Yorkville practitioner, remembered an emergency call one dark, cold stormy night. As he crossed a big marsh, the trail became so faint that he had to lead the horse while creeping along the ground feeling for a wagon rut. When he finally arrived, a man hollered from an upstairs window that the patient was better, he wasn't needed and warned the doctor to send no bill.

Dr. William B. Southard of Kalamazoo had a similar experience. Late one bitterly cold night in 1875, a messenger knocked loudly on his door to summon him to a woman who was so sick "she's going to die." After an eight mile drive over roads nearly drifted shut, and twice overturning the sleigh, he arrived at 4:00 a.m., nearly frozen. Once inside, the husband informed him "Well, you've been so long coming, my wife is better now and of course I can't pay you for the visit because she's pulling through without any medicine." Most doctors accepted such experiences as an occupational hazard. Occasionally, one got surprised by a bonus. Charles B. Hays, a prominent Kalamazoo realtor, walked into Southard's office one day and paid him for a long overdue account—his own delivery.

Despite experiences with deadbeats, many doctors demonstrated exceptional generosity and kindheartedness. Dr. Ezra Adams of Cooper rarely received settlement in full for any account. When strapped for funds, he sent word to a family to please send him $10 or $20. One woman responded that her husband drank up all the money and the children needed clothing, but he could have her sewing machine in payment. Dr. Adams sent both an apology for having asked and a receipt paid in full. Kalamazoo's Dr. George Britton not only performed a great amount of charity work but saved, in a special account, all Sunday fees for distribution to the needy.

Other area physicians somehow found time for a variety of community services. Dr. Henry F. Thomas served with Gen. George Armstrong Custer's 7th Michigan Cavalry during the Civil War. Following graduation from the University of Michigan, he set up practice at Allegan in 1869. He became a member of the Michigan House of Representatives in 1873, a State Senator in 1875 and president of the village of Allegan four years later. Dr. Orin Burroughs, a veteran of the Atlanta Campaign, served as president of the village of Galesburg, a school director, and county superintendent of the poor for twenty years. Another Civil War veteran, Dr. Milton Chase of Otsego, was a justice of the peace for seven years, a fire chief for ten years, a village marshall and at age 80, a health officer. Nearby Plainwell turned out to honor Dr. Cicero Stuck for his 28 consecutive years of service on the village council.

His patients remembered Stuck as particularly kindhearted and sympathetic. He hated to compute his services in dollars and cents. When needy patients mentioned payment he was likely to reply "Now, now, brother; I haven't asked you for it, have I?"

But even Stuck became exasperated at times. He

Kalamazoo's Dr. Harris Osborn made patients feel better simply through the use of his ebullient personality.

regularly treated a woman who periodically became hysterical by attempting to teach her self control. One day when he himself had been up for several nights and was exhausted and nervous, she threw a particularly spectacular fit. He grabbed a pail, pumped it full of cold water, dashed it over her and added, as he jumped into his buggy, "I guess that will hold you for awhile."

Malingerers drew little sympathy from horse and buggy era doctors. Dr. Rush McNair remembered one of the first cases he treated when he set up practice in 1887. A woman had long feigned epileptic seizures, usually convulsing herself into the arms of the nearest handsome gentleman. When Kalamazoo wives saw to it that their husbands avoided her, the theatrics stopped. Then one day she sent her daughter for young Dr. McNair. He arrived to find her with a badly swollen arm, but it was blue not red from inflammation. When McNair caught sight of a cord tied tightly around her arm he made his diagnosis. Telling her that it was a very bad case and unless relieved she might lose her arm he prescribed: "I had in my case a pill called 'Little Devils.' One was a dose and two induced diarrhea. I gave her two, and told her to take two every three hours until relieved." She never sent for him again.

But, for those genuinely ill, the old-fashioned doctor practiced a bedside manner that soothed, comforted and literally inspired recovery. Then as now, confidence in the healer was essential, and when the doctor said things were getting better they usually did.

Kalamazoo's colorful Dr. Harris Osborne had a style worth remembering. When he entered a home where there was despair he responded with special treatment. He'd tell a funny story, in a brogue for Irish families or in a different accent for other ethnic households. He'd thump out a cheering tune on the piano or parlor organ, and make up a humorous song for the occasion. By the time he left, a dish of colorful pills beside the bed and echoes of the doctor's optimistic counsel caused many a patient to forget his woes.

The 62-year-long medical career of Dr. Abraham Van Horne spanned the pioneer and horse and buggy eras. He started as a saddlebag doctor in Barry County shortly after the Civil War, and for three years never saw another physician. His predominantly rural practice made him adept at expedients. When he met a man on the road who wanted cough syrup, he went to a nearby sugar bush, partially filled a bottle with sap, added some soothing medicine for the throat and handed the patient his bottle of "cough syrup." He often doubled as a dentist and sometimes had a patient sit along side the road as he extracted a tooth. More than once he treated sick stock as well as humans.

Van Horne later relocated in Otsego and just prior to the turn of the century he recommended the area's first appendectomy. Dr. Rush McNair performed the daring operation. Residents became incensed when they heard that McNair had cut into a patient's abdomen—it just wasn't done. Luckily, the patient recovered, and the community accepted this concept of surgical treatment.

A shift in popular attitude toward surgery was but one of a variety of changes that marked the evolution of medicine during the era. The region's first women doctors, for example, had gained acceptance. Dr. Matilda Towsley became Kalamazoo's pioneer female doctor following her graduation from the Women's Medical College of Philadelphia in 1869. During her thirty-six year long practice she specialized in pediatrics. Diminutive Dr. Della Pierce joined her in Kalamazoo in 1893 and became very active, particularly in the treatment of women and children.

Some area women doctors became outspoken advocates for greater equality. Dr. Kate Lindsay of Battle Creek rose at a meeting of the Calhoun County Medical Society in 1889 to argue that she was not in accord with the opinion of most authors that "modern advanced education is responsible for the increase of female disease." She found it "difficult to understand the connection between pelvic congestion and a knowledge of mathematics and the natural sciences." Several of her male colleagues, however, thought her ideas "a little too far fetched" and that women had mistaken their vocation and "ought to get married instead of trying to get a higher education."

Kalamazoo area doctors initiated their own Academy of Medicine in 1883, and it soon became a vital force for improved education and professionalism among physicians. The final year of the 1880s also marked the beginnings of Kalamazoo's first hospital. Using a $5,000 gift from Bishop Caspar Borgess of Detroit, St. Augustine Parish priest, Father Francis A. O'Brian, converted an Italianate mansion on Portage Street into a 20 bed hospital. Eleven Sisters of St. Joseph arrived on July 5, 1889, to organize the institution. They appointed a medical staff of eight local physicians, including genial Dr. Harris Osborne as chief of staff, and Borgess Hospital opened on December 8th. Before the year's end, four patients were admitted. By 1899, Borgess Hospital cared for 233 patients including some 40 charity cases. The following year a handful of local doctors formed the Kalamazoo Hospital Association, which was reorganized in 1903 as Bronson Hospital.

Kalamazoo and the surrounding counties left the horse and buggy era to greet the twentieth century with a progressive spirit of adventure, a spirit that would soon make national medical history.

Galen Gets a Gas Guzzler

Dr. W. E. Upjohn, an early automobile owner, approaching Vicksburg, ca. 1902.

Dr. Edward Ames hand-cranked the little engine, tossed his medical bag up on the high buggy-type seat, carefully adjusted the spark lever until the motor chugged just right and eased his new Locomobile onto unpaved and dusty East Lovell Street. It was August 1, 1902, and Dr. Ames had just become Kalamazoo's first physician to use an automobile in his practice. It was a rather daring move for a 51-year-old man who had been a horse and buggy doctor since 1878, and it marked the beginning of the end of a colorful era.

From that point on doctors began retiring their "hay-burners." In the twentieth century Galen would get around in a gas-burner. Some were loath to give up the advantages of equine companionship and an occasional nap in a moving buggy, but automobiles were faster and more efficient. Dr. George A. Rigterink, a long time country practitioner in Hamilton, finally retired his spirited team during the summer of 1907 and bought a Buick touring car. He retained the horses for winter travel. He never did quite get the hang of handling an automobile, driving a car as though it were a horse. He burned out many a clutch by following the old horse trainer's adage "machinery can be made to see reason if only your resolve is strong enough." In Kalamazoo a high percentage of doctors soon jumped on the automotive bandwagon. By 1905 Dr. Ames had traded his Locomobile for a Knox, and several other local physicians also owned automobiles.

The city's first automotive event on July 15, 1905, featured a special "doctor's race" in their honor. Drs. Augustus W. Crane and Caspar K. LeHuis evidently got the racing fever and "scorched" out on the street to earn Kalamazoo's first traffic tickets. The speed limit was 8 miles per hour in the business district and 15 miles per hour in residential areas in 1905.

Other doctors rushed less impetuously into the

horseless era. The bicycle craze of the gay nineties spurred some physicians to try two-wheeled travel. "Wheels" proved ideal for house calls, at least within the city in decent weather. Local bicycle mechanic, Maurice Blood, invented a basket suitable for carrying a medicine case. Dr. Rush McNair remembered one hot summer night when Dr. Cornelius Van Zwaluwenberg raced his bicycle past him on an emergency call. He was clad in slippers and a nightshirt that waved behind him as he rode.

The passing of the horse and buggy era signaled other medical developments. The state legislature brought greater order to the profession through an act in 1899 for "the examination, regulation, licensing and registration of physicians and surgeons." On March 22, 1900, all the doctors in Kalamazoo County made quite a procession as they presented their credentials to the state medical examiner at the Burdick House. In 1907 the Kalamazoo Academy of Medicine first published a fee schedule. Office consultation ran from $1 to $5, physical examination $2 to $10, ordinary baby delivery $15 to $25, and treatment of venereal disease, double ordinary fees, payable in advance.

Major trends in the automobile era included increased specialization by area physicians and individual achievements that brought worldwide fame. Dr. Augustus W. Crane, for example, pioneered in the field of radiology. He had established a general practice in Kalamazoo in 1894, and the following year became the first city bacteriologist in Michigan. Wilhelm Konrad Roentgen discovered X-rays that same year and by March 1897, progressive young Crane had built his own primitive X-ray machine.

In 1898 he delivered "The Roentgen Ray in Disease of the Lungs" to the Kalamazoo Academy of Medicine, a classic paper that was extensively reprinted. As his flamboyant wife, Caroline Bartlett Crane, led national crusades for clean streets and meat

Dr. Fred Bonine and a group of patients posed before his Niles eye clinic in 1916 (Courtesy *Berrien Bicentennial*, James T. Carney, ed.).

inspection, Dr. Crane continued his pioneering work in radiology. In 1905 Drs. Crane and Pfahler first recognized that the X-ray caused skin reactions. Crane escaped the fate of many early radiologists, "the martyrs", who inadvertently gave themselves radium poisoning, by covering his x-ray tube with heavy shoe leather and using high lead content glass for fluoroscopy.

Dr. Crane earned international acclaim for his discoveries in the application of the X-ray to gastrointestinal diagnosis and his invention of the kymograph, the first X-ray instrument designed to study a particular organ, the heart. In 1929, Drs. Crane and John B. Jackson established the area's first out-patient X-ray services at Borgess Hospital. Dr. Crane also applied his inventive genius to non-medical areas. He patented, in 1914, for example, an electric starter for automobiles. By the time of his death in 1937, Crane's medical bibliography included more than forty publications.

Other area physicians gained fame for spectacular clinical achievements. Dr. John Harvey Kellogg had galvanized a tiny Seventh Day Adventist water cure, established in the 1860s, into the Battle Creek Sanitarium. Kellogg advocated sensible eating, exercise and hydrotherapy and in his spare time invented as health foods granola, peanut butter, and corn flakes. By the 1920s, thousands of run-down patients made an annual pilgrimage to the "San" for a bout of "right living."

Dr. Fred Bonine, who popular novelist Rex Beach termed a "modern miracle man" in 1935, operated an equally famous eye clinic in Niles. For over half a century, Bonine specialized in non-operative eye treatments. He graduated from the University of Michigan in 1885, where as a student athlete he set a world record for the 100 meter dash that stood for 35 years. Following post graduate work in Europe, he returned to his home town of Niles. As word of his medical acumen spread, thousands journeyed to the Bonine Eye Clinic for treatment.

Railroads dispatched "Bonine Specials" from Chicago, Indianapolis and other large cities, and long lines of patients daily extended down the street from the clinic. Bonine examined as many as 517 patients a day as they sat in rocking chairs propped in the right position by wooden blocks. Rich and poor were treated alike at the Bonine Clinic, no appointments, first come first served. Dr. Bonine charged $2 for the first visit and $1 for each subsequent visit, and the destitute received his services free. Despite his work load Bonine also served as mayor of Niles for six terms and as a member of the State Athletic Board of Control.

Meanwhile, Kalamazoo's medical facilities evolved to keep pace with changing technology and the developing community. In 1905, a building committee headed by Dr. William E. Upjohn increased Bronson Hospital to 46 beds. In 1920 it became affiliated with the Methodist church and in 1928 expanded in size to accommodate 111 beds. A decade later, despite the Great Depression, a second $350,000 addition opened.

Borgess Hospital grew by leaps and bounds. Major additions in 1901, 1903 and 1907 almost totally concealed the original converted mansion on Portage Street. In 1916 hospital authorities announced plans for a new facility located on 40 acres of land off Gull Road. The beautifully designed Tudor Gothic Revival structure opened on September 29, 1917.

A tragic influenza epidemic, which killed millions worldwide and more than 500,000 across the United States following World War I, tested the efficiency of the modern new Borgess Hospital. The Sisters of Saint Joseph responded with overwhelming courage and nursed the hundred of influenza patients that

Kalamazoo's first hospital "Old Borgess," was a converted Italianate mansion on Portage Street.

streamed into old and new Borgess Hospital. In Otsego, seventy-two year old Dr. Abraham Van Horne took care of more than 800 cases of influenza himself and lost only two patients.

As the jazz age roared to a climax new Borgess expanded to provide 280 additional beds and old Borgess closed in 1928. The following year ushered in the Great Depression, a decade of hard times for all. Despite the grim economic climate Borgess Hospital continued to pioneer in health care. The first out-state neurosurgical and neurological out-patient services, for example, became available to Kalamazooans in 1936 when Dr. Richard Upjohn Light opened his private practice on the top floor of Borgess Hospital.

Light, a great grandson of Dr. Uriah Upjohn, earned his medical degree from the University of Michigan in 1928. Next he studied brain surgery under the legendary Dr. Harvey Cushing at Peter Bent Brigham Hospital in Boston. In 1934, while a research assistant in surgery at Yale Medical School, Light introduced to the medical world a device able to electrically stimulate a normal animal's nervous system by remote control. The development of the cardiac pacemaker came as a later outgrowth of this discovery.

Light retired from surgical practice in 1946 due to development of a skin sensitivity that prevented him from scrubbing up. He remained active in experimental science, however, and played a prominent role in the testing of the Upjohn Company's Gelfoam, a gelatine sponge ideal for stopping bleeding during brain surgery. Light's multi-faceted career also encompassed pioneer aviation and exploration, leadership that revitalized Kalamazoo College during its dynamic growth in the 1950s and 1960s and a broad array of community service work.

During the late 1930s, Borgess Hospital allocated a small basement room for the mechanical experiments of an orthopedic surgeon with an inventive turn of mind. Dr. Homer Stryker's amazing gadgets, and the company he developed to manufacture them, brought international fame to Kalamazoo. Stryker had first set up a general practice in Alma following graduation from the University of Michigan in 1925. He soon moved to Kalamazoo where he became county physician. Beginning in 1936, he spent three years at Ann Arbor developing skills in his real interest, orthopedics.

When Stryker returned to Borgess, he applied his mechanical ingenuity to various medical problems. In 1936 the famous Stryker turning frame for moving patients with spinal injuries made its appearance. Next he invented a practical rubber heel for walking casts and a hip nailing board to handle the new method of treating hip fractures. In 1942 he patented an oscillating saw which removed casts without injuring the underlying skin. An over-the-bed frame to support limbs in traction, a grasping bar enabling patients to move themselves in bed, the circ-o-lectric bed and other inventions that revolutionized hospital care soon followed.

Stryker's inventions came in time to make life easier for thousands of wounded World War II veterans. Many area doctors also served on active duty during the war. By March 1943, 48 members of the Kalamazoo Academy were in the service. Only 33 general practitioners, mostly ranging in age from 60 to 80, remained to care for the home front. The local medical industry contributed mightily to the war effort as well. The Upjohn Company, for example, won the prestigious Army/Navy "E" award for production of sulfa drugs, penicillin and serum albumen.

Dr. Rush McNair, "dean of local doctors," donated a set of 500 surgical instruments from his collection to aid Russian military surgeons in October 1943. His death a year later ended 57 years of medical practice and philanthropy in Kalamazoo. McNair had paused in 1937 to consider the changes he had seen since his horse and buggy days:

The automobile heated to parlor warmth in winter, paved highways snowcleared, electric-lighted roads, turning night driving into that of day, have redeemed the doctor from the wilderness. Laboratories making for the doctor a multitude of researches with retort, microscope and X-ray; the electric cardiograms traced by the heart itself, the electric cautery knife that cuts deeply but draws no blood; the mechanisms that measure the metabolism of cells of the body...all these and more are arrayed to the doctor's aid.

Could McNair return for a glimpse of the changes wrought by the succeeding half century, he would scarcely believe his eyes. The scores of conquered diseases, wonder drugs, organ transplants and sophisticated equipment and procedures would baffle the old doctor. But if he looked past the technology and at the members of his beloved profession he might spot attributes that run as a common thread through the pioneer period, horse and buggy days, automobile era and into the age of nuclear medicine—dedication, love of humanity and the healing touch of a good doctor.

Stalking Michigan's First Celery Grower

Cornelius De Bruin, ca. 1870, was one of many aspirants to the title of being the first celery grower (courtesy Kalamazoo Public Museum).

K alamazoo's most glittering society had assembled in the grand ballroom of the Burdick Hotel on December 19, 1856, to honor the fire "laddies" who gallantly guarded the city from conflagration. Kalamazoo's distance from eastern society did not prevent local belles from consulting the hand-colored plates in their *Godey's Lady's Book* magazines and thereby mimicking the most current New York dress styles. Elegantly beribboned gowns, all the rage that season, featuring bare shoulders, wasp waists and enormous hoop skirts that swept the floor to guard against fashion's faux pas—exposure of the female ankle. No disgraceful "Bloomers" dared appear among this set.

Little did the distinguished couples who strode sedately toward the banquet table realize but that they would be immortalized as culinary pioneers that evening, that they would be the first in Michigan, some say all of America, to encounter the crunchy vegetable stalks known as celery. Thomas A. Ackerman, proprietor of the Burdick Hotel, long remembered their response to the foreign food. "How do you eat this stuff?" asked several. "How is it grown, in hothouses or out of doors?" queried another. One puzzled diner, evidently not detecting whether it was animal, vegetable or mineral asked, "Is it grown from seed?"

George A. Taylor, as the story goes, a Scottish immigrant who had established a nursery in the vicinity of Henderson Castle on West Main Street Hill the year before, had brought with him from the old country some celery seed. Having germinated the tiny seeds, transplanted the delicate seedlings eight weeks later and harvested Kalamazoo's original celery crop, Taylor had offered some free to Ackerman in order to introduce the vegetable to Kalamazoo's finest and thereby create a market. Despite their puzzlement those brave souls apparently liked what they tasted—although the record does not reveal whether they chewed it *au natural*, lightly salted the celery or perhaps some gastronomic genius then and there first spread the stalks with cream cheese. Taylor tried the experiment on another set of palates three days later, at a Democratic Party festival held at Firemen's Hall, with similar results. Heartened by celery's reception, Taylor planted more the following spring and thus established the foundation for an industry that by the 1890s would bring Kalamazoo national fame as "The Celery City."

Ah, of such stuff are legends made. Unfortunately this particular tradition, fondly perpetuated in history books, including one I coauthored in 1981, does not bear well the light of close historical scrutiny. Scots can be justly proud of originating golf, bag pipes, Shetland ponies, collies and haggis, but George Taylor most certainly did not grow the first celery in America or even Michigan. And the story of Kalamazoo society's initial encounter with celery implies a naiveté little becoming a county seat let alone the bustling metropolis it had become by 1856.

Literary references to celery, in fact, occur as early as the eighth century B. C. The "selimon" mentioned by Homer in the *Odyssey* is thought to be wild celery. Wild celery, indigenous to salt marshes in Europe and Asia, is a much more pungent and strong tasting relative of garden celery. It was used primarily as a flavoring in soups and as a condiment similar to parsley. Sometime prior to the 17th century cultivation of a garden variety of celery began, apparently in Italy. In 1629, John Parkinson, the royal British apothecary, wrote that "sellery" was a rarity in England. But in 1699 John Evelyn stated in his *Acetaria; or a Discourse of Sallets* (salads) that "sellery, for its high and grateful taste was ever placed in the middle of the Grand Sallet at the great men's tables as the grace of the whole board."

Tiling the muck was essential to prepare the field for celery culture.

Later British horticultural writers invariably gave directions on the cultivation of celery. For example, James Gorton's *The Practical Gardener and Gentlemen's Directory for Every Month in the Year*, published in London in 1769, offers detailed instructions to those who would grow celery for salads:

> This is the time, about the end of April to prick out (transplant) the young celery plants sown in February. Make beds three feet wide of rich light earth. Dry it well: break the earth fine, and rake the surface very smooth. Prick in the best plants at the distance of about three inches every way. Give them a moderate watering till they take root. Then at a month's end, plant a few of them out for good into trenches. I say a few, because these early plants will soon run to seed, after they are fit for use.
>
> Therefore it is the best practice to sow more celery seed in the first week of April, to succeed those sown in March; upon a small bed of rich, light earth, well cultivated. Sow the seed equally, but not too thick, and rake it in lightly, so that the earth may not cover it more than an inch. Over which fix a few hoops, with a mat to cover the bed from the sun; and water the celery now and then lightly, and the seed will grow more freely, and the plants rise well.

June, according to Gorton, was the time for the young plants to be "transplanted into the ground in trenches where it is to remain and be blanched." Blanching or bleaching in trenches, a process in which the stalks were shielded from the sun to render them white, crisp and succulent, continued widespread until about 1850 when growers realized they could achieve similar results with less labor by mounding soil next to the stalks or by placing cedar blanching boards on either side of each row for two weeks. These techniques were widely used in Kalamazoo celery fields well into the 20th century.

I am not certain when celery first crossed the Atlantic but the earliest gardening manual adapted specifically to American needs that I have examined, Bernard McMahon's *The American Gardener's Calendar* (Philadelphia, 1819) carries detailed instructions for celery culture very similar to Garton's. Thomas Fessenden's popular *The New America Gardener* (Boston, 1828), which ran through eight editions in six years, also offered full information on celery. He noted that "the blanched leafed stalks are used raw, as a salad, from August till March, they are also stewed, and put in soups." Fessenden listed the varieties usually cultivated in America: "White solid, Rose-coloured solid, Italian, and Celeriac," The latter was a turnip type plant in which the root only was eaten.

Robert Buist's 1847 publication, *The Family Kitchen Gardener,* which soon became the recognized authority, named additional varieties including Giant Red, Giant White, Seymour's Red, Seymour's White and Lion's Paw Celery. The giant varieties, according to Buist, produced stalks four feet long! Buist also commented on celery in general: "This vegetable is yearly gaining repute, and is cultivated to a great extent..."

The pioneers who flocked to Michigan in the 1820s and 1830s came predominantly from New England and New York and they carried with them libraries containing some of the previously mentioned gardening manuals. Early American cook books also offer evidence of a general knowledge and appreciation of celery. The earliest I have seen, *The Universal Receipt Book* (Philadelphia, 1817) by sensibly named Priscilla Homespun includes a recipe

Kalamazoo promoted itself as the "Celery City" to the nation in prints such as this illustrating a Dutch grower in 1910.

for mixed pickles containing celery.

The 16th edition of Lydia Child's *The American Frugal Housewife* (Boston, 1835) gives advice on preserving the vegetable through the winter: "Celery should be kept in the cellar, the roots covered with tan (bark) to keep them moist." Catherine Beecher's *Housekeeper's Receipt Book* (N. Y. 1845) included two recipes for celery vinegar made with the seeds as well as "Celery Sauce for Boiled Fowls:"

> Take four or five celery heads, and cut up all but the green tops into small pieces, and boil it in half a pint of water till tender. Mix two teaspoonfuls of flour with a little milk and put in, with a saltspoonful of salt, and butter the size of an egg. When it boils, take it up.

Incidently, a saltspoonful equals 1/4 teaspoon and butter the size of an egg, depending on how the hen is laying, is roughly two ounces.

Eliza Ann Wheeler in her *The Frugal Housekeeper's Kitchen Companion* (N. Y., 1847) suggested:

> Celery makes an excellent addition to salads—gives an agreeable flavor to soups and sauce, and is sometimes stewed as an accompaniment to boiled or stewed meat. Wash six or eight heads, trim off the outer leaves, cut the heads up in bits 3 or 4 inches long, stew them till tender in a half pint of veal broth; then add two spoonsful of cream, and an ounce of butter rolled in flour. Season with pepper, salt and nutmeg, and simmer the whole together.

Lettuce, watercress, celery, endive, etc. "are employed as salads" wrote Dr. Russel Trall in his *New Hydropathic Cook Book* (N. Y., 1853). But Trall, one

South Burdick St.
Kalamazoo, Mich.

This view of South Burdick Street, ca. 1910, shows the bustling "Celery City."

of pioneers of the health food movement later advocated so ably by Dr. John Harvey Kellogg of the Battle Creek Sanitarium, thought those salad plants "too strong and acrimonious to be healthful; and those who avoid strong, rank animal foods, and eschew alcohol and tobacco, can hardly desire them. The lettuce tribe are injurious on account of containing the narcotic juice from which opium is made."

If , as we have seen, celery was far from a curiosity in America, what about the Michigan scene in particular? A group of the state's leading gentlemen farmers, including several from Kalamazoo, met on March 7, 1849, and founded the Michigan State Agricultural Society. Governor Epaphroditus Ransom of Kalamazoo was elected president. The society held its first state fair on September 25-27, 1849, in Detroit. Among other familiar garden vegetables, the Society offered a $2 prize for the best six heads of celery. Although it is not known who if anyone won the award, J. C. Holmes of Detroit definitely exhibited examples of the alterative Seymour's Solid Celery and William Y. Patterson from Springwells, now part of Dearborn, displayed another variety. Even closer to Kalamazoo, George Hentig won a prize of 50 cents for the celery he exhibited at the Calhoun County Fair on September 20 and 21, 1849.

Three years later Jeremiah Brown, from Battle Creek, published instructions on how he grew celery. He noted that it was "not only delicious but very healthy, and it gives such an air of gentility to the dinner table, all genteel people should certainly cultivate it." Officials of the Kalamazoo County Fair, in fact, offered a 50 cent premium for the best six stalks of celery in 1853, two years before Taylor immigrated to Kalamazoo. Previous to 1856, the Hillsdale, Jackson, Genesee, Shiawasee, Washtenaw and Oakland County Fairs also reported celery exhibits.

George Taylor, then, could not have grown the first celery in America or Michigan and it seems highly unlikely even in Kalamazoo. In all fairness to his memory, it appears that his son, James Taylor, contributed the account of his father's vegetable feat sometime previous to 1887 when the first printed record of the legend appeared. Later historians have based their version on that source. Taylor, it should be noted, is also only one of a dozen more contenders for the title of pioneer celery grower. The passing of each old celery grower, in fact, seemed to spawn new accounts of his precedence in the industry.

Regardless of who first grew it, it was definitely the Kalamazoo Dutch immigrants who excelled in celery culture. By the 1890s, at the height of Kalamazoo's celery fame and when the city's rail shipments of the crunchy vegetable gave it a freight rating second only to Detroit, the Dutch had taken complete control of the industry. They brought to celery growing an agrarian wisdom learned over the centuries as the Netherlands reclaimed its land from the sea. They also were able to buy cheaply small plots of swampland eschewed by earlier settlers, which proved to be rich muck, ideal for celery culture. The large families they raised also brought success in the extremely labor intensive business.

Not surprisingly, various early Dutch growers are frequently credited as planting the city's first celery. Next to George Taylor or his son, James, or a mysterious Taylor named Walter, Cornelius De Bruin is most often cited. The story as told by his son, Marinius De Bruin, was that his father emigrated from the Netherlands with the intention of establishing a seed business. One day while walking through a garden located at the corner of Cedar and Westnedge "he spied a queer looking plant growing in the soup celery bed." From that genetic anomaly he developed

A common sight during Kalamazoo's celery heyday was crates of celery being loaded into box cars.

the famous Kalamazoo variety of celery which he began to commercially raise in 1866. Unfortunately, this story loses some of its credibility because Marinius De Bruin was not born until 1867, hence he obviously relied on hearsay. A good number of sources , incidentally, credit Marinius De Bruin as the first grower as well as Lendert De Bruyn.

John De Kam wrote a latter from Missouri claiming that it was he who first grew Kalamazoo celery in 1866 "on an alley running from Burdick Street to a creek (Arcadia) 5 or 6 hundred feet." The seed had been brought from Holland by L. De Bruyne, who also helped him grow it.

An article in the April 24, 1890, issue of the *Kalamazoo Gazette* gives a new and interesting twist to celery's origin. It seems that in 1857 a Gerrett Remsinse made a study of the local conditions, cleared a field on South Burdick Street first planted celery seeds. Unable to market his first crop of the strange vegetable, he fed it to the hogs.

Other contenders for the celery crown came fast and furious. When John Steenard died on September 9, 1899, a *Gazette* obituary announced that he had arrived in Kalamazoo in 1854 and grew the first celery. Andrew Oliver, a Scot, died on November 21, 1918. His obituary claimed he grew the first celery offered for sale in Kalamazoo. He, however, would have been only seven years old in 1856. Other sources credit J. F. Farnum and J. C. Newland with the honors.

Then there is the case of the sole celery queen claimant. A copy of an obituary notice from the Columbus, Ohio, *Dispatch* of an unknown date announces the sad demise of Mrs. Pauline Marie Othelia Nitschke, a royal name if ever there was one. Daughter of a soldier who fought at Waterloo, Mrs. Nitschke was born in Silesia in 1830. At a young age she immigrated to America, settling first in Milwaukee, then Detroit and finally Kalamazoo "where she cultivated for the first time the celery plant and proved its adaptability to the soil." She soon moved to Columbus and apparently her pioneer contribution had been forgotten by all but her.

My personal favorite, however, appears for the first time in a *Kalamazoo Gazette* article on celery in 1925. It seems that "nearly 70 years" before an employee of the Kalamazoo State Hospital "experimenting in his spare moments with plants and garden seeds, found that the black muck lands so conspicuous around Kalamazoo at that time, contained the elements necessary to successfully raise celery here." But alas, "the discovery failed to arouse any particular interest among the natives of the village and the identity of the discoverer was soon lost." Nevertheless, the vegetable, as a result of this unknown celery pioneer's efforts "was grown and served on the table at the Michigan Asylum for several years before people started raising it on a larger scale."

Setting aside the fact that the State Hospital did not open until 1859, this version has great appeal. Picture a kindly old attendant, briar pipe in mouth, seeking respite from Bedlam by puttering in his celery garden. Envision him carrying double armfuls of crispy Seymour's Giant Celery, the four foot stalk variety, to the Asylum kitchens to be served up to patients who might well have asked "How do you eat this stuff?"

But to return to reality. Whodunit? We will probably never know for sure. Perhaps it is all academic anyway. We will also never know who grew Kalamazoo's first goobers, horseradish, mangel wurzel or kale. But then Kalamazoo was never "Kale City" to the nation.

Father Nicholas Sifferath: Forgotten Missionary to the Ottawa

The Rev. Sifferath grew his long beard because a doctor told him it
would help his poor eyesight.

The branches of the great pines sagged low under the shroud of snow draped across the northern woods inland from Cross Village. The wilderness of white lay silent save for the faint crunch and creak of snowshoes and the heavy breathing of a small black hooded figure struggling through the drifts. The Rev. Nicholas Louis Sifferath's long reddish beard had frosted stiff. Periodically he paused to wipe his fogged spectacles. Then, in a clearing ahead, the priest spied his destination, a shanty, seven or eight feet square, crudely woven of sticks and branches.

A set of tracks led to a crawl hole at the side of the hut. The spry little priest bent low and peered into the interior. As his eyes adjusted to the dark he discerned an ancient Indian woman sitting alongside a small fire, intent on roasting a slab of flesh she had hacked from a dead horse.

Softly, kindly, Sifferath spoke in Ottawa to the *Nokomis*, told her of his religion and pleaded with her to allow him to baptize her. She listened for some time in silence then turned her furrowed leathery face to the intruder—her eyes snapped angrily in the firelight. No! She would not renounce her native beliefs for that of the white man. She had resisted for nearly half a century, since Father Pierre Dejean had first established a mission in the L'Arbre Croche region in 1829—most of her people had given in—her friends and her own children—but not she!

For some time Sifferath continued to calmly talk to her, about her earthly misery and her eternal soul. Then he arose, shrugged his shoulders and turned and walked away. Despite the squalor he had seen, he could not help but think the old woman seemed happy, contented. That visit was but one of many he paid the *Nokomis*, always showing her kindness and pleading with her to accept baptism. Stubbornly she refused, growing angry each time the priest talked of his religion.

130

Sifferath paused for a few seconds and looked up from the lectern. Suddenly, he was no longer among the Ottawa and Ojibwa in the north woods of Michigan. He was in a warm auditorium and before him stretched an audience of nuns and fellow priests at St. Joseph Academy in Adrian. Seeing that all eyes were open and full of interest, Sifferath continued, in his thick German accent, his recollections of the Indians:

Then the old woman went once to see a friend in another village, and while there became very sick. Her friends exhorted her not to refuse any longer to be baptized. But she, in the first place, did not listen at all, but became angrier. They said again to her, "Why are you so very obstinate refusing to be a Christian?" saying to her, "All your friends, the Indians, are good Christians now a long time,but only you and a few others refuse the grace of baptism, and perhaps you shall die pretty soon, and if you are not baptized before you die, you shall be unhappy yonder for all eternity. Make up your mind, therefore, and be baptized." And in that way they exhorted her, and then the sick old woman commenced to cry, saying this to her friends standing around her: "Well then, if you fetch for me that little priest who was all the time so good to me, if he comes, that priest shall baptize me." And then they said to her, "That priest you speak of is 12 miles away from this place; but there is one priest only six miles from here, that one we shall fetch for, because the road is very bad to fetch the little priest." And then the sick woman said "No, only that little priest shall baptize me." Then they came and told me all that the woman said and then I went there, baptized her, and she was glad and very contented, and she became well from sickness and lived five years

Harbor Springs area Indians stopped their logging operation to pose for the camera, ca. 1890.

longer, dying a Christian. I related this fact to you because in order to prove that the Indians remember their benefactors.

Sifferath knew well the native peoples he had lived with for more than 20 years. A biographical article printed in Kalamazoo newspapers at the time of his death in 1898 noted:

His contact with the red race almost made him lose his identity and he became to a great extent an Indian in his manner and custom. His mode of living for the greater portion of his priestly life made him peculiar and eccentric, and unfitted him for parish work among white people.

A strange little man who had shed the veneer of society for a less fashionable albeit more natural life style, who had gone to the Indians to bring change and instead been changed himself, Sifferath seemed an embarrassment to his contemporaries and to the Church. It was easy to shunt the eccentric into unimportant positions when he had prematurely worn himself out from his strenuous work. And while thick volumes have recorded the exploits of other Catholic Indian missionaries such as Bishop Frederick Baraga, the history books have ignored Sifferath entirely or relegated the rudiments of his career to a footnote. Yet his lecture on the Indians, hand copied by Sifferath in a notebook in 1883, offers a rare glimpse, by a sensitive and sympathetic observer, of a vanishing culture. It and the life of its author merit a better fate than to be forgotten.

Born into a family of prosperous farmers on December 12, 1828, at Bickendorf, Germany, located near the ancient city of Thrier, Sifferath received a liberal education from his parents. After serving a short stint as a jeweler's apprentice he decided he had a higher calling. Like many another European youth, he thirsted for adventure among the wild Indians of North America. "Animated with the missionary spirit" and armed with a substantial advance inheritance, Sifferath sailed for America in 1852. He made his way to Chicago, undoubtedly via the Michigan Central or the Michigan Southern railroad, both of which reached the city that year. There he joined his brother Philip who had proceeded him.

In Chicago, Sifferath came under the influence of Reverend John Baptist Weikamp, a native of Westphalin, Germany, who had come to the city in 1850. He had built a frame church, St. Francis Assisium, on the north side for the use of the third order Franciscan community of which he was superior. As colorful and eccentric as his young countryman who yearned to carry the cross to the Indians, Weikamp would earn his own controversial niche in the annals of northern Michigan.

Sifferath continued his education in Chicago and he also taught a parish school there for two years. By 1855, Weikamp had grown weary of the city and determined to reestablish his mission in a more rural setting. He traveled to Sault Ste. Marie in October of that year, where he consulted with Father Frederick Baraga, bishop of the newly created Apostolic Vicariate of Upper Michigan. Delighted at the prospect of receiving much needed assistance in his far-flung frontier responsibilities, Baraga offered to cede Weikamp a tract of land he had recently purchased at the present site of Petoskey. There he was invited to reestablish his Franciscan society, which then numbered ten lay brothers and 11 sisters. Baraga was particularly pleased that two of Weikamp's brothers desired to become missionaries.

Weikamp wasted little time in closing his church in Chicago, placing it for sale and leading his flock to a new life in the north country. On November 28, 1855,

The Rev. John Baptist Weikamp posed in a Napoleonic manner which revealed his personality.

Baraga paid a visit to Little Traverse Bay where at L'Arbre Croche and the nearby missions more than 1800 Catholic Indians dwelt. Baraga recorded in his diary, "I met, to my great joy, Reverend Fr. Weikamp who had arrived only a short time before." Ten days later, Sifferath and Philip Seraphim Zorn, a German brother three years his junior, took the first steps toward priesthood when Baraga clipped their hair in tonsure and granted them minor orders.

Baraga ordained Zorn as priest on January 20, 1856, and assigned him to assist Father Lawrence Lautishar in the L'Arbre Croche Mission, at the present site of Harbor Springs, where Baraga had himself begun his career in northern Michigan in 1831. Sifferath would not be ordained until August 23, 1857. In the interim he remained with Weikamp and also spent considerable time in Baraga's home in Sault Ste. Marie, studying under the bishop and learning the Indian languages.

Despite the benefits of gaining two priests to assist him, Weikamp's removal to Little Traverse Bay would prove a mixed blessing to Baraga. Weikamp did not care for the site originally offered him by Baraga and instead purchased a peninsula curving into the bay at Harbor Springs which later became the exclusive resort of Harbor Point. But that location proved too confining for the grandiose institution Weikamp projected. In 1856, he purchased, with the assistance of a share of Sifferath's advance inheritance, 2,000 acres of land 16 miles to the north at La Croix, later renamed Cross Village.

There Weikamp and the band of monks and sisters who had followed him to the north country established the Benevolent, Charitable and Religious Society of St. Francis. Soon after their arrival they began the construction of a large wooden structure which became known as the Cross Village Convent. An imposing building consisting of a large main auditorium flanked by wings on either side, it was laid out so that the villagers who worshipped in the center and the nuns in one wing and the monks in the other could all see the altar but no group could see the other.

Soon a grist mill, saw mill, various shops and other structures and a parochial school for Indian children were added. Later came a small hospital and an Indian orphanage. The Cross Village Indians performed most of the construction work under Weikamp's supervision. The society thrived as the brothers cleared land, planted crops and raised livestock. The convent became a self-sufficient feudal community surrounded by palisades, producing practically everything used there from the wooden shoes worn by the nuns to its renowned currant wine.

Despite Weikamp's efficiency and zeal in establishing his monastery, he brought Bishop Baraga considerable trouble. On January 23, 1856, Bishop Anthony O'Regan of Chicago wrote Baraga:

> I am told that Reverend Weikamp, for many years a priest of this diocese, has been received into your diocese. You must be aware that he had no letter, no dimissory from me, his legitimate bishop. I have not released him from the obligations he owes me. He did not even ask to be released from them. He did not even comply with a single duty, that a good priest respects. He has violated all the statutes of the Church in this country. He built a church, for which he collected money in Chicago, and I am told, that he got monies for this purpose from the religious societies of Europe. This church he now retains and offers for sale, as private property. He has it locked up. I have withdrawn it from the use of religion. This is a large congregation without any other place of worship. This conduct we cannot allow and I am sure, Right

Rev. Bishop, that you will not countenance this priest until he restores this property to its legitimate use and until he has in his favor the commendation of his ecclesiastical superior.

When Baraga discussed the matter with Weikamp, he found him adamantly convinced of the justice of his actions in Chicago. For more than two years Baraga continued to try to convince Weikamp to do the right thing to no avail. Finally realizing his persuasions would have no impact on the stubborn German priest and that the society could be of great assistance to him, Baraga blessed the church and consecrated the cemetery there during a tour of his missions which brought him to Cross Village on June 1, 1858.

The cemetery consecrated by Baraga contained a bizarre structure which further demonstrated Weikamp's eccentric nature. Shortly after he arrived at Cross Village, Weikamp had his own sepulchre constructed. It consisted of a deep cellar, walled with masonry and surmounted with a small wooden building, kept securely locked.

Inside the crypt stood Weikamp's casket, decorated with a skull and cross bones. Each day, the priest walked to his tomb where he spent three or four hours meditating beside his casket. He also frequently repaired to his macabre sanctum to read books and newspapers and for his after dinner smoke.

Needless to say, the Indian villagers soon concocted their own explanations of Weikamp's weird behavior. Some claimed his "private cellar" contained casks of choice wine with which the priest fortified himself. Others believed it to be the rendezvous of a mysterious rich woman from Germany who purportedly had funded Weikamp's American ventures.

Beyond Weikamp's morbid preoccupation with

Weikamp's Cross Village Convent was protectd by a palisade.

his own demise, there were other indications that all was not right at the Cross Village convent. The superior, according to the recollections of a number of the villagers gathered in the late 1920s by Marie Trostheide, a relative of Sifferath's, was a tyrant who ran his monastery with an iron hand. He meted out severe punishments, including flagellation, to any of his followers who dared to so much as speak to a member of the opposite sex or who failed to follow any of his other stern dictums. John Chippewa, an old Indian who had attended Weikamp's school as a boy, remembered the priest as "a mean old pup, mean to the sisters and brothers."

Whether Weikamp was deliberately cruel or simply a Prussian attempting to maintain discipline the best way he knew is open to conjecture. However, kind-hearted Sifferath broke away from his superior not long after the move to Cross Village. That parting of the ways may have been aggravated by Sifferath's insistence on Baraga's ordaining him rather than Weikamp. Finally, in 1861, Baraga also could no longer tolerate Weikamp's irregularities and he suspended him as pastor of Cross Village. He would continue to remain there as superior of his monastery until his death in 1889, however. A rival and smaller mission situated on the high bluff overlooking the lake continued under Baraga's jurisdiction.

In the meantime, following his ordination in 1857, Sifferath was assigned briefly to the Indian mission on Mackinac Island from which he also tended a small mission at Cheboygan. Then, Baraga reassigned Sifferath to Harbor Springs as an assistant to Lautishar. After training Sifferath, on June 14, 1858, Lautishar followed his childhood pastor from his native Austria, Rev. Francis Pierz, to Minnesota. Sifferath then took charge of the Harbor Springs mission. Baraga paid a visit there a week later where, he noted in his diary, "the good humble Fr. Sifferath serves God."

Lautishar would meet an untimely fate in his quest "to labor among the pagan Indians of Minnesota." He established a mission on the shores of Red Lake, north of present day Bemidji in August, 1858. The following December, at the request of a band of Indians living on the other side of the lake, he crossed the ice and instructed them in the catechism. Returning alone in late afternoon, he got caught in a fierce blizzard. Blinded by the flying snow and sleet, he stumbled about for several hours until his legs froze and he could no longer walk. He finally laid down on the ice and perished.

On the June 1858 tour of his missions during which he finally relented and blessed Weikamp's church at Cross Village, Baraga also stopped at Harbor Springs. He described Sifferath as "a conscientious, zealous, and pious priest, who in a short time has learned the Indian language tolerably well and daily perfects himself in it." In company with Sifferath, Baraga visited the small Indian missions at Sheboygan on the west shore of Burt Lake and Bear River, later renamed Petoskey, where the bishop preached.

Sifferath remained at Harbor Springs until 1863, when he traded places with his fellow Franciscan brother turned priest, Zorn, at Cross Village. Despite the opposition of his old adversary Weikamp, Sifferath enjoyed some success there. In the fall of 1864, Baraga again conducted a two month tour of his missions. At Cross Village he:

...was very much pleased at the progress made since my last visit. As the church was too small, the Indians determined to build an addition and fit it up. They executed the work so beautifully and durably that no white carpenter could have done it better. It is true, the zealous missionary, Rev. Louis Sifferath, helped them at it considerably. In order to animate the Indians, who are naturally slothful, to work, he himself put his hands to the work and encouraged them more by example than by work to labor assiduously at enlarging their church.

Sifferath, who perhaps knew the true Indian character better because he lived as one of them, would undoubtedly have respectfully disagreed with his bishop's statement concerning the Indian's "natural slothfulness." He defended them in his 1883 lecture:

> I hear sometimes a saying among white people, that the Indian men make their wives do the work, and that they smoke their pipes, doing nothing but watching their wives working, and compelling them to work and bear hardships. That is not true, as concerning the Ojibwas and Ottawa Indians. These Indians work together, man and wife, but the man will always do the heaviest work, so as to spare his wife, and the wife is very happy and contented, working that way with her husband. Whenever they have to do some work, they assist one another, as I observed many times by seeing them working.

Sifferath also found the Indians very charitable, giving and caring in a manner that would put many white Christians to shame:

> The Indians are very good for assisting one another. When any one of them is sick for a long time, or burned out, or in any other misfortune whatsoever, so that he cannot help himself any more, in that case all his fellow Indians come together to assist him. Then in the time of planting they sound the trumpet in the morning to bring them all together, then at about nine or ten o'clock

Graves at the Indian cemetery at Cross Village were marked by gaily decorated wooden crosses.

they all go, men and women, to the field or garden of that sick, disabled, or unlucky person, Then all together they work, planting, making, or repairing the fence, working that way all day, sometimes two or three days, joyfully and faithfully, and so they do the same way when one of them is burned out, or his house or property is destroyed by fire. Then they come, all the men Indians together, working, building up again the house of the person who was burned out. And so working and assisting one another, I have seen them do that very often, they do much charity among themselves, loving, helping, and giving food to the poor, who are not able to work.

Whenever the Indians help one another, as I related just now, they work all together, commencing about ten o'clock, then they come together to rest awhile, and taking their dinner all together, having prepared something for it in every house, they carry it in baskets to the woods and the garden, where the assembled workers are working for charity's sake. And then they sit down for dinner, on the ground and in a circle together, and eat that food which was brought for them from the village houses, and during the time that they eat they look very happy, conversing with one another very peaceably. After the dinner they smoke their pipes, lying on the ground for a while, and after that smoking they commence their work together in the same way, until about five or six o'clock in the evening when they stop and go home. And then at home they relate to their friends who stayed home how they labored through the day.

In the same way they rebuild a house for their neighbor if he has been burned out. Everyone gives something to buy the materials needed to finish the new building. And so in all distress they assist one another, especially do they assist the sick among them, giving them what they need and visiting them, doing charity for them in the very spirit of the true Christian, so, they love one another, pitying and consoling their afflicted fellows.

The Indian culture Sifferath documented in his lecture had, in fact, already undergone a great deal of transition from its aboriginal state. Centuries of contact with succeeding French, British and American fur traders, as well as Catholic and Protestant missionaries, had resulted in a hybrid culture which retained many of the old ways but which also melded new ideas into distinctive Indian traits. For example, the religious holiday of Epiphany or Twelfth Night, which marks the close of the Advent season on January 6 of each year, had long been celebrated in England and France. Among its traditions was the baking of a large cake in which a bean had been placed. When the cake was cut and divided among the guests of a fancy ball, the person who received the piece containing the bean was the king for the celebration. Sifferath described an Indian version:

Every year, the Indians, about New Years, make two suppers. At the first supper they put a bean in a fried cake and then put that cake with the bean in a large dish full of cakes, mixing them all up together at the table, and then, by eating them at the first supper, that person who is so lucky or unlucky to get the cake which contains the bean, must contribute or procure victuals or food for the second meal, as much as he can, and so the same way they do again at the second meal or supper, as they call it, as they did for the first supper. They prepare or cook in every house something for that meal, and then they, from every house, carry their prepared food to one of the largest wikiwam, Indian house, where they all come together, men, wives and children, young and old persons, in order to partake of that supper which is always about four or five o'clock in the evening. At the time of the supper, they come together, standing in crowds around that house selected for the supper, because the house is not large enough for them all at one time to eat at the table. So therefore they set the table again and again, until they all have partaken of their contributed supper. At the first supper only those partake or eat who are the most respectable among them.

Sifferath also documented another festive custom, the christening of white visitors with an Indian name:

Whenever a white person, man or woman, comes to live among them, then they make a contributed supper, just the same way I related before. They make all their meetings suppers or meals, when meeting all together. Then, they invite the white person, who came to live among them, to come and take supper with them during their meeting or convention. And then, during the supper, that white person eating with the Indians, the chief proposes an Indian name for that white person, and then all the other Indians at the supper cry out, pronouncing that new name in their Indian language. Then the chief leaps up on his chair, leaping and singing in the old Indian fashion, some of the others assisting him, singing for a short time. Then, after that supper, they all go home, taking their dishes and other things to carry home. Yes, I saw them very happy on these occasions.

One reason why the Indians appeared so happy during those christenings was because it gave them an opportunity to use their subtle sense of humor to get the last laugh on those white men who exploited them. John C. Wright, a turn-of-the-century poet and chronicler of Indian lore in the Harbor Springs vicinity, recorded one such example.

It seems that one of the leading merchants of Harbor Springs, a tight wad who often cheated the Indians in trade, had asked to receive an Indian name. Accordingly, the Indians held a feast accompanied with much jollity similar to that described by Sifferath. Then they announced the merchant's new name—"Bub-big."

He was proud of his honor, liked the sound of his name and lost no time in informing everyone in Harbor Springs of his new appellation. Finally it occurred to him to inquire what the name meant. When he asked the first Indian who entered his store what Bub-big meant he was promptly told it meant flea. He was not quite so proud of his Indian name after that. Nevertheless, it clung to him for the rest of his life.

In his lecture, Sifferath discussed many other facets of Indian culture, funeral and burial customs, gardening, sugar making, the constructs of porcupine quill decorated wares by the women, etc. He concluded by saying:

> They have their own ways of living and shall always continue in it, as long as any Indian is in existence. But still they are good and peaceable people, and also good in many respects, and they are good Christians. Now my dear friends you have heard something about the Indians, all that I said was facts, and the very truth, because I have seen it with my own eyes, lots of times, during the 20 or more years that I lived among them, and also because I conversed and talked to them in their Indian Language, hardly using any other language during 20 years except books.

Weikamp's bizarre tomb became a tourist attraction.

Sifferath became very adept at the Ottawa and Ojibwa tongues, which were similar. In 1864 he secured Baraga's approval to publish an Indian catechism he had translated into Ottawa. Not until 1869, however, would he succeed in having the 64 page pamphlet printed in Buffalo. Apparently not widely disseminated, it has become a rare collector's item.

For five years Sifferath struggled along at Cross Village, enlarging the church somewhat while receiving little financial assistance from outside the impoverished community. Those of the villagers, white and Indian, who found Weikamp's institution objectional patronized his little church, located on the steep bluff overlooking Lake Michigan, near the ancient wooden cross which had given the village its name. Although the monastery overshadowed Sifferath accomplishments, his little mission was vexing to the superior. Weikamp apparently nursed a hatred for the bearded little priest who had dared defy him. The beard itself was a matter of contention. Weikamp, who was clean shaven, believed it improper for a priest to wear a beard. But Sifferath defended his hirsute appendage, stating that a doctor had recommended it as a remedy for his weak eyesight.

As long as Baraga remained bishop, there was little Weikamp could do to remove the sacerdotal thorn in his side. But in 1868 Baraga died. The lower Michigan Indian missions which had been transferred to Baraga's jurisdiction when he became bishop of the Upper Peninsula Diocese in 1853 reverted back to the custody of the Detroit Diocese under Bishop Peter Paul Lefevere. Lefevere conducted an inspection tour of the northern Indian missions in the fall of 1868. There is no record of what actually transpired when he visited Cross Village but apparently Weikamp's thriving operation impressed him far more than

149

Sifferath's struggling little mission. In any event Lefevere ordered Sifferath to transfer to another assignment and to shave his beard. When Sifferath refused, Lefevere suspended him and the mission was officially closed. While continuing his circuit of the northern missions, Lefevere fell while stepping into a canoe and seriously bruised his ankle, an injury which resulted in his death the following March.

Although his official sanction had been removed Sifferath continued to minister to the Indians he so loved. He maintained his headquarters at Cross Village and periodically canoed or walked across the ice to Beaver Island, Garden Island, Mackinac Island, the Fox Islands and the Les Cheneaux Islands. He constructed seven chapel for the indians at those remote sites, doing much of the labor himself. Most of what he received for support consisted of corn, maple sugar and other Indian foods. He supplemented those by hunting and fishing. Sifferath became more and more like an Indian.

Then in 1877 tragedy struck. Sifferath's brother Philip had remained with Weikamp's monastery. One of his responsibilities was to drive the convent's herd of cattle to pasture in the morning and back to the barn in the evening. One day the herd wandered into the deep woods and he could not locate them. Twice during the night he returned without success, and then, according to local lore, before being sent out the third time he was horsewhipped.

A few days later, Sifferath learned that his brother had not returned from the woods. In company with a pair of Indians he searched for two days, before finding his brother's body hanging from a beech tree in the woods near Levering. They carried the body back to Cross Village where Sifferath buried it near his little church on the bluff. Weikamp refused to allow his burial in the Society's cemetery since he, apparently, had committed suicide. Whether he had hung himself as a result of the shame of the horsewhipping or despondency caused by Weikamp's cruelty or that he was murdered was a much discussed mystery that remains unsolved. Eventually, however, his body was disinterred and reburied in the mission cemetery.

The tragedy of his brother's death took a toll on Sifferath's health, which had never been robust. Later that year, Bishop Caspar Borgess, who had succeeded Lefevere as head of the Detroit Diocese, charitably reinstated Sifferath as a priest and transferred him to Detroit. The missionary still had his beard and he kept it, too. During the following two decades he served as chaplain in various institutions including St. Joseph's Retreat in Dearborn, the Academy of the Sacred Heart at Grosse Point and St. Joseph's Academy at Adrian. Despite "the eccentricities" which the bishop thought rendered him unfit for regular parish duties, he made many friends who relished the kindly old missionary's stories about his adventures among the Indians.

In 1889, Rev. Francis O'Brien established Kalamazoo's first hospital named Borgess in honor of his friend the bishop who had given $5,000 to start the project. As early as 1892, O'Brien, often a friend to needy priests and who was deeply interested in Michigan history, had invited Sifferath to transfer to Borgess Hospital where he could serve as chaplain and have a comfortable home and be taken care of. In feeble health, five years later he was ready to come, not to Borgess Hospital, but to the newly established mother home of the Sisters of St. Joseph at nearby Nazareth.

Sifferath arrived at the Michigan Central Railroad Station in Kalamazoo on September 14, 1897. His entire worldly possessions consisted of seven dollars in cash and a small trunk containing his memorabilia, papers and books, chiefly multiple copies of his Indian

Father Sifferath just prior to his death in 1898.

catechism.

At Nazareth Academy Sifferath valiantly conducted the morning service each day. But after three months his health had deteriorated to the point that he was placed in Borgess Hospital. He died there on March 10, 1898, his beard, now snowy white, intact. His body was conveyed to Detroit's Mt. Olivet Cemetery where he had purchased a grave site in 1885. At Nazareth, succeeding generations of Sisters of St. Joseph carefully preserved in their archives the photographs, clippings and manuscripts, including Sifferath's 1883 lecture on the Indians, which document the life of the gentle little missionary who spent his last days among them in Kalamazoo.

But what became of Sifferath's nemesis— Weikamp? After he had apparently bested Sifferath and secured Cross Village all to himself, his monastery prospered, gaining considerable renown, particularly for the wine bottled there. Weikamp continued to enjoy his daily visits to his own tomb. As the monk grew older, he spent more and more time meditating each day in the crypt. Finally, feeling a premonition that he had not long to live, he called the members of his society together and instructed them regarding his burial.

A few days later, following a drive in the country, his horse became frightened and Weikamp was thrown from his carriage, suffering severe internal injuries. An old friend, unnamed, but according to John C. Wright, "known as a man of sterling qualities and utmost reliability," hastened to Weikamp's sick bed. Wright quotes the friend's occult experience in *The Crooked Tree,* published in 1917:

Father Weikamp and I had been, since our acquaintance a few months after his arrival at Cross Village, on very intimate terms. I felt considerable pride, I must acknowledge, in knowing that I was one of the few in whom he seemed to have real confidence. He often invited me to the convent and even asked me upon several occasions to accompany him to his sepulchre or underground vault. I always gladly accepted these invitations, partly at first, I will admit, from curiosity; but also on account of genuine friendship. While in the little room upon my last visit I remember distinctly Father Weikamp telling me of his firm conviction and belief in a future life. He was rather eloquent in his statements and I was struck with his sincerity. We conversed at length upon the subject, and as I was about to go, I suggested to him that whichever one of us should die first would, if within his power, manifest himself to the other in some manner, He readily consented to this proposition and seemed pleased with the idea.

When I learned of his last illness I was at a distant point on urgent business, but started immediately for his bedside to see him once more if possible before he passed away. After a long ride, I reached the convent late at night and in order not to cause any undue disturbance, I decided to hitch my horse temporarily while I went to the door to find out whether I had arrived too late or was yet in time to see my friend. I remembered that a little distance beyond the convent, in the direction I was travelling, there was a little sheltered arbor and hitching post beside the roadway where I had sought refuge once before, and in going thither I glanced toward the sepulchre which was now within my view. To my astonishment I saw a light issuing therefrom. As soon as I reached the arbor I hitched my horse hurriedly, and started across lots towards the sepulchre, to see what was taking place at that late hour. As I neared the little building, I could distinctly hear Father Weikamp's voice alternately singing and praying. The door was flung wide open and looking in I beheld him on his knees as I had seen him many times before. I could not have been mistaken—I was too well acquainted with that short, rotund figure, and full, red face surmounted by a fringe of white. I, of course, concluded that he had recovered from his illness and not wishing to disturb him, quietly withdrew to the convent, where I knocked at the door and was admitted by one of his sisters of the society. I told her I had come hurriedly from a distance to see Father Weikamp knowing that he had been very ill; but was glad to see that he had recovered.

"Indeed," said she, "the good Father died several days ago and was laid to rest in his sepulchre yesterday."

"Impossible!" I exclaimed; "I was just there and saw him kneeling in front of his coffin as usual."

"We will go and see if any strange thing has taken place," said the nun, who called another, and accompanied by the two I returned to the sepulchre.

When we arrived there all was dark; the tomb was securely locked, with absolutely no signs of any living thing within. To satisfy my curiosity the sister, who remembered me well as a friend of Father Weikamp, unlocked the door and we entered with a lighted lantern. All was still as death and everything in its proper place. The lid of the coffin containing Father Weikamp's remains was firmly fastened and appeared to have been neither moved nor molested. We opened the casket, to more thoroughly convince ourselves regarding the matter, and beheld the familiar features of the dead tertiary, whose body was in precisely the same position in which it had been placed the day before by the members of the

Benevolent, Charitable and Religious Society of St. Francis.

Following Weikamp's demise, his monastery fell into disorder. It was disbanded in 1894 and the property sold. Time and the elements took their toll on the many structures and little if anything remains today to mark Weikamp's Cross Village empire.

A fire in 1918 burnt to the ground most of Cross Village, including Sifferath's home and little chapel on the bluff, and the community never regained its former stature. In 1948 some non-Indian residents of Cross Village pulled the crosses from the graves in the Indian Cemetery and moved Weikamp's body from its tomb to that cemetery. Wycamp Lake, northeast of Cross Village, perpetuates the tough old friar's name, if not its correct spelling—kindly Father Sifferath's has all but been forgotten.

Civil War Belles and Battles

Julia Wheelock, educated at Kalamazoo College, served as a hospital agent during the Civil War.

Uncle Tom's Cabin—John Brown's Raid—Abraham Lincoln elected president—South Carolina secedes—the seige and bombardment of Fort Sumter—and suddenly the greasy smoke of battle shrouded a nation at war with itself. On April 15, 1861, Lincoln called for volunteers to resist the "insurrection." Michigan responded with enthusiasm, mass patriotic rallies, bombastic speeches denouncing the rebellion—and thousands of men rushed to join the colors. Eventually over 50% of the state's military age male population would serve.

In the fall of 1861, the 2nd Michigan Cavalry was being organized in Grand Rapids under Lt. Col. William Davis and Major Robert Minty. Twenty-year-old William Carlisle of Edwardsburg in Cass County enlisted with Company L of the unit at Niles. His cousin, Orville Carlisle, from Buchanan, followed him into the same company. Then Ashley, Orville's 19-year-old brother, ran away from the family homestead in Buchanan to join Company L with his kin.

But not for long. Daniel and Hannah Carlisle rushed to Niles and dragged their youngest son back home. A few days later he ran away again—back to the regiment. At that point Hannah Carlisle announced, "If my youngest is going to war, I am too," and she did. She followed the 2nd Cavalry when it left Grand Rapids for St. Louis in November. She helped cook for the regiment, took care of washing and when some of the soldiers became ill she began nursing.

Then in March 1862, Col. Philip H. Sheridan assumed command of the regiment. Tradition has it that Sheridan took one look at the long line of civilians following his troops and put his foot down, telling Ashley, "No boy's going to war with his mother tramping along." Hannah was forced to leave the 2nd Cavalry. Nevertheless, she was determined to serve elsewhere. She entered the hospital service and received a commission as a regular Army nurse. Stationed in the post hospital in Columbus, Kentucky, until the war's end, she became a superintendent in the Freedmen's Department, organized to assist emancipated slaves for an additional year. She finally returned home to Buchanan in July 1866, where she joined the local Grand Army of the Republic (GAR) post.

Hannah Carlisle died in 1906 and was buried in Oakbridge Cemetery in Buchanan. Next to her official government tombstone with its iron GAR flag holder stands that of Ashley, her youngest son. He made it through the war, having fought in the Atlanta Campaign with the 2nd Michigan Cavalry and returned to live in Buchanan until he died in 1929.

In August of 1862, Robert Bruce Wallace, a farmer in Burlington Township, Calhoun County, enlisted in Company C, 19th Michigan Infantry. He was 29, his wife Mary 24. They had a two and a half year old son and a six month old baby daughter. When he left, the full responsibility of managing their 160 acre farm rested on Mary's slim shoulders.

The 19th Michigan was organized at Dowagiac under Col. Henry Gilbert of Coldwater, Lt. Col. David Bacon of Niles and Maj. William R. Shafter of Galesburg, who would later win fame as commander of the American expedition to Cuba during the Spanish American War. On September 10, 1862, Mary heard that the regiment was about to leave Dowagiac. She took the train for maybe a last farewell to her husband. Her diary entries record her experiences:

> September 12. We went to Dowagiac—arrived about five o'clock. Bruce was taken with an ague (malaria) chill on the cars. The tavern was crowded so we had to go to a private house—stayed all night.
> September 13. We all went over to the camp

ground—the soldiers were formed in line on dress parade. The Governor came. They marched to their speaking ground. The governor delivered a speech. I did not go. I went to the tent with Bruce. I put a pocket in his overcoat. We stayed all night on the camp ground. We got a tent for our own folks. Bruce got some medicine for his ague. Bruce handed me thirty dollars, his bounty money.

September 14, Sunday. Bruce is some better—the soldiers were ordered to get ready to march by 4 o' clock in the afternoon to the cars. They started on the cars about 5 o' clock for Ohio.

Then she was back on the farm—hard at work—without a man to help her manage the back breaking routine. She recorded:

September 16. I gathered wood—done chores—boiled soap. I cut a pole to draw water with...I turned Harrison's pigs out of the corn field and fixed the fence all around the field.

September 17. I gathered wood, boiled soap, pulled weeds, hoed turnips and baggas and got Mr. Harrison's pigs out of the corn two or three times.

September 18. I turned the calf in the north corn lot. Mr. Harrison's pigs got in my soap grease in the swill—wasted it—also in the corn 3 or 4 times. I went along the road and stopped the fence where I thought a pig could get through.

September 19. I went and borrowed Mr. Rowe's shovel, emptied the leach, put a barrel of new ashes back in the leach, carried the shovel home, borrowed his cutter, cut corn—drove Harrison's pigs out of the corn—cut 10 shocks of corn—drove the pigs out again—drove them home—carried the corn cutter home.

When the never ending round of farm chores, and Harrison's pigs, permitted, Mary worked at finishing the new house they were building and she nursed her baby.

And so it went—hard work and battles with nature—to say nothing of pigs. Until May 1863 when Bruce returned, wounded. He had been shot through both shoulders in the Battle of Thompson's Station, Tennessee, where the 19th Michigan had made a desperate stand against Gen. Earl Van Dorn's cavalrymen until after five hours of furious fighting and out of ammunition the Michigan men surrendered.

Mary Wallace and Hannah Carlisle served their country in different ways. Their stories typify the diverse participation of Michigan women during the Civil War.

But in developing a roster of Michigan heroines it is important to begin with the decades prior to the war. It was the abolitionists whose relentless campaigning focused the nation's eyes on the horrors of slavery. Here Michigan women took an active roll.

Elizabeth Margaret Chandler, a Quaker, had begun contributing anti-slavery poetry and essays to Benjamin Lundy's abolitionist periodical, *The Genus of Universal Emancipation,* at the age of 18. She made special appeals to women, encouraging them to take their place alongside men in the fight against slavery. In 1830, the 23-year-old reformer moved from Philadelphia to a farm near Adrian, Michigan Territory, and from that remote location she continued her influential anti-slavery writing. In 1832 Chandler held a meeting in the small Quaker settlement in Lenawee County and organized the first anti-slavery society in Michigan. Unfortunately her brilliant career was cut short two years later when she did of a fever.

Chandler's work was carried on by another Lenawee County Quaker woman, Laura Haviland.

"Aunt" Laura Haviland holding slave irons.

Charles and Laura Haviland had moved to a farm in Raisin Township in 1829 and both became active in the abolitionist movement and other reform causes. In 1837 they opened a school for orphans on their farm which ultimately became the River Raisin Institute—a preparatory school open to all regardless of sex or color—as well as a haven for fugitive slaves bound for Canada. When Haviland lost her husband, parents, a sister, and her youngest child to an epidemic in 1845 she threw herself into the center of anti-slavery activities in the northwestern state. She became an operative in the Underground Railroad and despite a reward of $3,000 on her head, traveled many times through Ohio, Indiana, and Michigan assisting slaves into Canada. Her autobiography, *A Woman's Life Work*, records scores of exciting adventures and near escapes.

During the war she visited army hospitals and prison camps and in 1864 became an agent for the Michigan Freedmen's Aid Commission. In 1879 she went to Kansas to assist the ex-slaves who had flocked there.

She was closely associated in that effort with yet another Lenawee County Quaker abolitionist, Elizabeth Comstock. She had become actively involved in the underground railroad following her emigration from Canada to Michigan in 1858. She toured the northern and border states delivering fiery speeches at Quaker gatherings. When the war broke out she continued to travel, promoting abolition, peace, temperance and women's rights. In October 1864, she met with President Lincoln and they engaged in a Quaker type prayer meeting.

Lincoln had a visit from another famous Michigan woman lecturer that same month—Sojourner Truth of Battle Creek. Sojourner had spent the first 30 years of her life as the slave of a wealth Ulster County, New York, Dutch patroon. She ran away in 1827, the year prior to the emancipation of slaves in New York. She soon replaced her slave name, Isabella, with Sojourner Truth and began to preach a mystic religious doctrine. Her tall, gaunt, masculine figure and guttural Dutch accent attracted attention. By the mid 1840s she had become an enthusiastic abolitionist crusader and later she campaigned for women's rights and temperance. Her personal magnetism drew large crowds who were awed by her wit, down-to-earth remarks, gospel songs and gift for repartee. For example, one day before a crowd:

George Goodrich of Milton, Wisconsin, chided "Aunty Sojourner" for smoking a pipe even though she spoke for temperance. "The Bible says nothing unclean can enter the kingdom of heaven. A smokers breath is unclean," he scolded. Continuing her puffing, she commented, "Brudder Goodrich, when I go to heaven I plan to leave my breff behind me."

In 1856 Sojourner Truth moved to Harmonia, west of Battle Creek, and later to that city—where she became one of the area's most flamboyant and best loved citizens. When she died in 1883 her funeral was the largest Battle Creek had ever seen.

But most Michigan women led less dramatic lives than the abolitionists. They bore their part of the war through suffering and worry, saw their husbands, brothers and fathers off, wrote cheery letters and scanned newspaper accounts of battlefield casualties—while managing life without their men the best they could. Some became active on the home front, knitting socks, rolling bandages and holding "Sanitary Fairs" to raise money and supplies.

In 1863 a band of young Kalamazoo women formed the Alert Club to call on homes and solicit promises of donations. Lists of pledges were turned

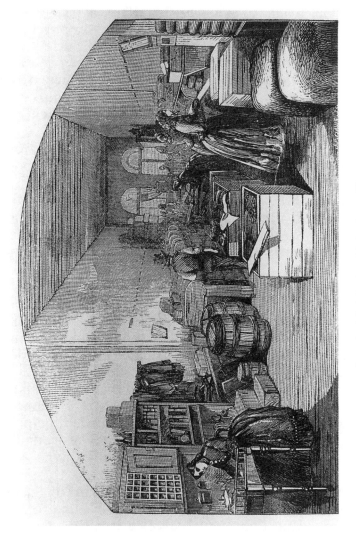

A typical Soldier's Aid Society office.

over to their brothers, The Minute Men, who picked up the goods in wheel barrows and wagons and delivered them to Soldiers Aid Societies.

A great deal of food was sent from Michigan for sick and wounded soldiers—barrels of apples, firkins of butter, kegs of pickles, plus money to buy other delicacies. The Michigan Soldiers Relief Society was set up to provide liaison between Michigan soldiers and their families and to distribute gifts sent from home. Several "lady agents" were employed to visit hospitals, locating and providing for the Michigan wounded.

Julia Wheelock attended Kalamazoo College from 1858-60 and then taught school in a one-room country schoolhouse near Muir in Ionia County. On September 10, 1862, a neighbor girl burst into the classroom bringing news that Julia's brother, Sgt. Orville Wheelock of the 8th Michigan Infantry, had been seriously wounded in the Battle of Chantilly, Virginia.

Julia and Orville's wife, Anna, hastened to Washington, but Orville was dead and buried before they arrived. While in the capital they appealed to the Michigan Soldier's Relief Society for help in getting Anna a widow's pension, and Julia Wheelock decided to remain and work for the organization.

She spent the remainder of the war as a hospital agent, visiting hospitals and military camps, distributing presents to Michigan wounded, helping write letters to home, holding the hands of wounded homesick boys and in general assuming much of a nurse's role.

Women nurses of the Civil War were, in fact, quite different from those of today. There was no formal nursing education available—it was all on the job training. Despite the efforts of the famous nurses of the war, Clara Barton, Mother Mary Ann Bickerdyke and Dorothea Dix, most surgeons refused to allow female nurses to take an active part. Their role was that of cook, laundress, to help hand feed the wounded and to offer the healing maternal power that was felt to be a natural attribute of women.

When the war began, Dorothea Dix went to Washington and offered her services to the surgeon general. Because of her reputation as a humanitarian reformer, he commissioned her with the duty of organizing a corps of female nurses. Washington was besieged with all types of women wanting to be nurses but Miss Dix had distinct ideas as to the type of woman needed and issued a circular:

> No woman under 30 years need apply to serve in government hospitals. All nurses are required to be very plain looking women. Their dresses must be brown or black, with no bows—no curls or jewelry, and no hoop skirts.

Unfortunately for the wounded, most photographs of her nurses seem to fit this description.

Dix was concerned with maintaining proper morality and preventing scandals that might discredit the whole profession of nursing. She promptly declared war on the nurses who had followed the regiments. With the backing of the secretary of war she had many of the original regimental nurses removed—but if they fit her austere standards they were transferred to Army hospitals.

A number of women from Michigan served as nurses under these restricted circumstances. Some were initially motivated by the same patriotic fervor that sent their male counterparts to enlistment stations.

Mary Penfield left her home on Academy Street in Kalamazoo in April 1862 to become one of the first Michigan women to go into regular hospital nursing. She served at Paducah, Kentucky; Lake Providence, Louisiana; and at Vicksburg, Mississippi. She returned to Kalamazoo in January 1865, physically worn out from nearly three full years of hospital service.

Julia Loomis De Quindre, a Battle Creek widow in her early 30s, decided she would become a nurse in 1862. She entered the Army hospital at Chester, Pennsylvania, that summer where she had charge of providing medicine and special dietetic needs. She served in various Army hospitals throughout the war and compiled one of the longest service records of any Michigan nurse.

When the war began, Rena Littlefield was a 19-year-old schoolteacher in Sturgis. She desperately wanted to get into the action. Since neither her father nor brother could go she determined to represent the family herself. When the Sanitary Commission refused her request to enter hospital service because of her youth, she stubbornly applied again and again until the commissioners agreed to give her an appointment if she could persuade six older women to join also. She got the six, though all but one deserted. Littlefield finally got her appointment any way and served until the war's end.

Janette Maxwell from Lawton enlisted with the 6th Michigan Infantry at Kalamazoo in August 1861. Col. Frederick Curtinus appointed her as hospital nurse and ordered she be provided transportation and one meal ration per day. She stayed with the regiment until April 1862 when she became a Dix nurse in Washington. She recorded a poignant experience she had there:

> While passing through the ward I came upon a youth who looked as though his place were in the schoolroom rather than as a soldier. When he saw me watching him he broke down completely, and cried like a child. My own tears mingled with his as I tried to comfort him. I learned that he was not sixteen when he left his widowed mother in

168

Civil War nurses, as pictured in this contemporary engraving, were robust ladies.

Kentucky and started for the front, and that night was the first time in eighteen months that he had heard a woman's voice.

Mary Blackmar was a medical student at Hillsdale College when the war began. She elected to serve her internship in the field rather than at a hospital. Her recollections, penned in 1901, testify to the primitive field hospital conditions as well as her example of almost superhuman dedication:

> After one of the fearful onslaughts at Petersburg, the wounded came pouring into my tent, which was nearest to the firing line, so that the drummer lad had named it "the Half Way House." One lad dropped from the wagon in which he was being transported as they passed my tent. I ran and cried out to the driver. He coolly replied, "He is dead, what does it matter!"
> I knelt by the boy's side and found a remote evidence of life, but hemorrhage was so profuse it seemed he could not survive. I called the attention of surgeons, but all said "We must go on." So with my knowledge that life was not extinct, and that he was so young and had the force of youth, I remained on the ground at his side not daring to leave him, but compelled to use my fingers as a tampon. I remained with him twenty-four hours before I felt safe in having him carried to a ward. Cramped and exhausted from such a strain, in addition to weakness induced by loss of sleep through nights and days previous, I could hardly crawl into my tent.

Blackmar was later put in charge of the Confederate wards—where she became a third Michigan woman to have an experience with Lincoln. Lincoln and Grant were inspecting the hospital when, as Blackmar recalled:

> I heard General Grant say distinctly, "These are the
> Confederate quarters." President Lincoln
> immediately said, "I wish to go in here alone!" I
> drew myself up into the corner as close as possible,
> and he bent under the open flap and came in. He
> went at once to a bedside, and reverently leaned
> over almost double so low were the cots, and
> stroked the soldier's head, and with tears
> streaming down his face he said in a sort of sweet
> anguish, "Oh, my man, why did you do it?" The
> boy in gray said, or rather stammered weakly,
> almost in a whisper, "I went because my State
> went." On the ground floor, so quiet was the
> whole ward, a pin could almost have been heard to
> fall. President Lincoln went from one bedside to
> another and touched each forehead gently, and
> with tears streaming asked again the question, and
> again heard the same reply. When he finally
> passed out from those boys, some gray and
> grizzled, but many of them children, there came as
> from one voice. "Oh, we didn't know he was
> such a good man! We thought he was a beast."

Still other Michigan women, like Hannah Carlisle,
followed their husbands or sons into the service to be
with them. In May 1861, when George Van Pelt of
Coldwater enlisted as sergeant major in Battery A, 1st
Michigan Light Artillery, the Loomis Battery of
Perryville fame, his wife Mary enlisted with him as a
nurse. Except for a brief period spent in a regular
Army hospital Van Pelt's wife stayed with the
regiment in camp or on the march. Only when her
husband was killed at Chickamauga did she return
home.
Similarly, when Hiram Hinsdale of Detroit enlisted
in Company D, 2nd Michigan Infantry, his wife Jane

171

"took not kindly to the idea of remaining at home while her husband went away to be shot at, and the more she thought of it, the less she liked it. She decided it was her place to nurse him if he fell and if not, then his comrades should have her services," and she left with the regiment. After the battle of First Bull Run, despite the fact that the 2nd Michigan was one of the few regiments that retreated in good order, Jane Hinsdale lost track of Hiram and went searching for him among the wounded on the battlefield. Confederate Cavalrymen captured her, carried her back to Manassas Junction, locking her in a old barn with 30 or 40 wounded Union soldiers. Among those was a Dr. Taylor of the 6th New Jersey Infantry who had gathered important military intelligence which he copied onto scraps of newspaper. Jane got an interview with Gen. Pierre Beauregard, persuaded him to let her go, and with his pass made her way back to the Union lines, barefoot. She delivered the vital scraps of newspaper to Gen. Joseph Mansfield. Eventually she found her husband alive at Arlington Heights. She stayed near him, serving as a nurse, until his enlistment ran out and they both returned to Detroit in June 1864. Congress awarded her a pension of $12 a month in 1891.

The 2nd Michigan Infantry seems to have been particularly fortunate in the number of colorful females associated with it. Annie Etheridge became "the daughter of the regiment." She performed courageous first aid work on the battlefield. When the regiment went into line she filled her saddlebags with lint and bandages, stuck a pair of pistols in her belt, and galloped on horseback to the front. At the 2nd Battle of Bull Run, Etheridge was kneeling by a soldier, binding his wounds, when she looked up to see Gen. Philip Kearny on horseback beside her. He said, "That is right, I am glad to see you helping these poor fellows and when this is over, I will have you

Sarah Edmonds, alias Franklin Thompson, disguised herself as a male
slave to spy behind Confederate lines.

made a regimental sergeant." Unfortunately, Kearny was killed two days later before he could award Etheridge her promotion, although she later received the Kearny Cross for valor.

When the 2nd Michigan Infantry went west in 1863 Etheridge transferred her allegiance to the 3rd Michigan Infantry. When most of the men in that unit headed home at the end of their reenlistment in June 1864 she transferred along with those who reenlisted to the 5th Michigan Infantry. When the 5th mustered out in Detroit in July 1865, Sgt. Daniel G. Crotty wrote:

> Noble Annie is with us to the last, and her brave womanly spirit breaks down, and scalding tears trickle down her beautiful bronze face as each of the boys and comrades bids her good-bye.

Congress voted Etheridge a $25 a month pension in 1887.

Yet another female member of the 2nd Michigan Infantry vied with Etheridge in terms of her colorful exploits. She was Sarah Edmonds, alias Franklin Thompson. Edmonds had grown up in New Brunswick, Canada. She ran away from home in her teens, disguised as a boy, to escape a marriage her father had arranged. Evidently liking that disguise, she kept it. Taking a name to match, Franklin Thompson, she got a job selling bibles for a Hartford, Conn. publishing firm. Just before the war Thompson moved to Flint, Michigan, where her friends thought of her as: "a good looking, likable, successful young man, who made money, dressed well, drove his horse and buggy, and had many lady friends."

When the war began, a friend, William R. Morse, organized the Flint Union Greys, which became Company F, 2nd Michigan Infantry, and Thompson enlisted as a private. Physical examinations were not then required. By June 1861 she was on her way to the front in Virginia where she fought at Blackburn's Ford, First Bull Run, and in the First Peninsular Campaign of 1862. Part of the time Thompson was on hospital duty, but she also served as brigade mail carrier, and as an aide to Col. Orlando Poe during the Battle of Fredericksburg. On at least two occasions she volunteered for spy duty behind Confederate lines, once disguised as a woman! Most of her comrades never discovered her true sex. One recalled years later that "he was a whole-souled, enthusiastic youngster, frank and fearless." But at least one comrade, Jerome Robbins, shifted from he to she when referring to Thompson in his diary entries.

When the 2nd Michigan was transferred to Kentucky in the spring of 1863 Thompson deserted. She later claimed that she had contracted a severe fever and thus faced hospitalization and discovery. But contemporary evidence from two diaries suggests that she had fallen in love with James Reid of the 79th New York Infantry who also resigned at that time. In any event, Thompson, now Edmonds again, moved to Oberlin, Ohio, resumed female attire and eventually went to work as a nurse. She wrote a semi-fictional account of her adventures, *Nurse and Spy in the Union Army,* which was published in 1865 by the same Hartford firm for which she had earlier sold bibles. Her book became very popular and was reprinted several times under variant titles.

After the war, Edmonds married a carpenter, Linus Seelye, and moved to Charlevoix and eventually to La Porte, Texas, where she was mustered into the local GAR post. In 1884 she was placed on the Army pension roll at $12 per month.

There were many other interesting Michigan women participants of the war, including Elizabeth Lucas from Saginaw, Betsey Cook from Jackson, Susan Lovell from Schoolcraft, and Bridget Deavers, an Irish lass known affectionately as Michigan Biddy, who rode into battle with the 1st Michigan Cavalry.

But the Michigan woman who won the most contemporary fame was Major Pauline Cushman. She, along with Belle Boyd, became the only Civil War era female spy to be enshrined in the *Dictionary of American Biography.*

Pauline Cushman was born in New Orleans in 1835. Soon after, her father moved his large family to Grand Rapids where he became an Indian trader. When Pauline had grown into a beautiful, Kent County teenager, according to her contemporary biographer, Ferdinand Sarmiento, a local Indian chief, Leaping Thunder, fell in love with her. To win her heart he killed many buffalo and fought a fierce battle with a rival tribe in a narrow mountain pass.

Now these feats would have been a little hard to do in Michigan in the 1850s but Sarmiento was writing for eastern readers used to thrilling dime novels.

His description of Cushman's appearance does not ring particularly truthful either, especially when compare to her likeness in the volume's frontispiece. He wrote that she was:

> ...lavishly endowed with the wealth of nature, her form is perfect—so perfect that the sculptor's imagination would fail to add a single point, or banish a single blemish. Her arm is equally beautiful, resembling in mold the marble efforts seen in the great art galleries of Europe. The outlines of her face are of exceeding beauty, and the perfect features are set off to the best possible advantage by a pair of large, flashing black eyes.

Fortunately, Cushman fled to New York City before Leaping Thunder could claim his well earned prize. Naturally, once there she was immediately hired

This plate from Pauline Cushman's 1865 biography illustrates her rescue by Gen. Rosecrans at Shelbyville, Tenn.

as an actress. March of 1863 found her playing at a theatre in Louisville, Kentucky, and that was the beginning of her great adventure. A pair of paroled Confederate officers offered Cushman $300 to make a pro Southern toast during a performance. She reported this to the local provost marshall who suggested she make the toast and use it to launch a career as a union spy.

Cushman toasted Jeff Davis that night, got fired from the cast, and gained a reputation as a southern sympathizer. Then she was commissioned as a secret agent with instructions to penetrate into the South and collect all the military information possible but not to make notes or maps. At Shelbyville and Tullahoma, Tennessee, however, the temptation became too great and she made careful drawings of Rebel emplacements, which she hid in her shoe soles. Having this information on her made her nervous, so nervous that when she was routinely questioned she panicked and tried to escape. She was captured, searched, and the papers found. Her captors took her to Gen. John Hunt Morgan, who though reputedly enamored by her beauty passed her on to Gen. Nathan Bedford Forrest. He confronted her with her probable guilt and passed her on to Gen. Braxton Bragg who told her brusquely, "You'll be hanged—that's all."

During her ten-day-long court martial she sickened and when the court found her guilty and sentenced her to be hanged as a spy she completely collapsed. Before hanging her, the Confederates, always gallant, nursed her back to health—but before the sentence could be carried out Bragg had to suddenly evacuate Shelbyville before Gen. William Rosecrans' advancing army and Cushman was left behind. She related her intelligence report to the first Union officers who found her and that information proved valuable to the Army of the Cumberland as it moved through

Tennessee.

Pauline Cushman returned north, to be lionized as a symbol of patriotism, as the "lady spy of the Cumberland." Lincoln commended her, she was formally proclaimed a major of cavalry and permitted to wear the symbols of her rank. She returned to the stage wearing her officer's uniform and toured the nation lecturing on her deeds. This high point of her life was brief—inevitably audiences wearied of the lady spy of the Cumberland. Following the war she headed west still lecturing in uniform and embellishing her exploits with each telling.

Her life went downhill. She married a succession of Californians, became a drug addict and died from an overdose of morphine in 1893. The San Francisco G. A. R. escorted her flower laden casket to the veterans section of the city cemetery, a squad fired a volley over her grave and a bugler sounded taps for the most flamboyant of the Michigan Civil War heroines.

Michiganians can be rightly proud of the more than 90,000 men from the state who served in uniform during the Civil War. But the part played by their sisters—who defied the customs and prejudices of the era to take their ranks on the homefront, in the hospitals, in the battlefield and behind enemy lines—is also a heritage worth remembering.

When Passenger Pigeons Darkened Michigan's Skies

Frank Leslie's popular magazine featured passenger pigeon hunting prints in the 1850s.

As the spring dawn tinged Grand Traverse Bay pink the passenger pigeons began to stir. Cooing farewell to mates and squabs in the nest, the advance flights of males whirred from the roost, stretching some 20 miles along a tract of dense timber blanketing the center of the Leelanau Peninsula.

Lord, they were beautiful birds! Males sported reddish orange rimmed eyes and legs, brownish red breasts like robins, bright slate-blue backs and wings. Covered with a gorgeous rich metallic iridescence, their necks shimmered with the hues of the rainbow. Similar in shape to a mourning dove, passenger pigeons were nearly twice as large. Females were somewhat smaller and less striking in their plumage.

Pioneer conservationist John Muir, whose family had emigrated from Scotland to the Wisconsin frontier where he grew up in the 1850s, recalled in his autobiography the impression made on him by the first, wild pigeons he saw: "Oh, what colors! Look at their breasts, bonnie as roses, and at their necks aglow, wi' every color juist like the wonderfu' wood ducks. Oh, the bonnie, bonnie creatures, they beat a'! Where did they a' come fra, and where are they a' gan? It's awfu' like a sin to kill them!"

Chief Simon Pokagon, an educated Potawatomi from Berrien County known as "the Longfellow of his race," wrote in 1895: "It was proverbial with our fathers that if the Great Spirit in his wisdom could have created a more elegant bird in plumage, form and movement, He never did."

Beautiful and swift, able to fly from 60-80 miles per hour, passenger pigeons existed in enormous numbers. In 1813, ornithologist John James Audubon observed a Kentucky flight pass overhead so dense that "the air was literally filled with pigeons; the light of noonday was obscured as by an eclipse; the dung fell in spots, not unlike melting flakes of snow; and the continued buzz of wings had a tendency to lull my senses of repose." That flight of pigeon continued to fly overhead at a rate of 60 miles per hour for three days without cessation!

Although single birds weighed less than a pound, so many pigeons roosted together in single trees that their combined weight often sent great branches or entire hardwood giants crashing to the ground. When the millions of birds left a nesting site, the forest floor lay carpeted with six to eight inches of droppings.

While gigantic flocks once ranged across much of America east of the Rocky Mountains, by the last half of the nineteenth century relentless persecution by hunters had driven the birds to take refuge during nesting times in the Great Lakes region. It was primarily in Michigan and Wisconsin that the passenger pigeons made their last stand.

The literature abounds with recollections of Michigan pioneers and sportsmen who marveled at the wild pigeons' beauty, speed, numbers and delicious taste. One of the most sensitive accounts was penned by Etta Smith Wilson, who grew up at Northport in the Leelanau Peninsula during the 1860s and 70s. Her father, a full blooded Ottawa named Payson Wolf, had married one of the daughters of the Rev. George Nelson Smith. Smith had relocated his Old Wing Mission to the Northport vicinity when, not unlike the pigeons, his Indian followers were pushed out of northern Allegan County by the arrival of the hordes of the Rev. Albertus Van Raalte's Dutch colonists. Wolf was a skilled pigeon hunter. Over a half century later his daughter remembered vividly his technique.

At dawn, when the first birds began to speed arrow-like from the roost, Wolf strode to the brow of a steep ravine a few yards from his house while an assortment of his dozen children scampered behind, lugging big wicker clothes baskets. Wolf cradled a huge double-barreled muzzle loader in his right arm.

A powder horn and shot flask swung at his side. Having poured an unmeasured handful of powder down the barrels which was wadded and tamped down followed by another unmeasured handful of bird shot also wadded and tamped, Wolf awaited the flocks which would nearly darken the crisp morning sky.

Suddenly, they came with a roaring rush and he fired both barrels at once into their midst. The birds "rattled down around him like a double handful of gravel." Reloading as fast as he could he shot again and again into the flock, pausing only when his gun became so hot he faced the danger of a premature discharge. When the gun cooled down he resumed his firing. Frequently he felled 70 birds with each blast and once he brought down 124 birds with one shot.

Soon the other inhabitants of Northport, alerted by the tocsin sound of Wolf's shotgun grabbed their firearms and scrambled to the top of the hill and began blasting away as fast as they could. Still the pigeons continued to fly by the thousands through that terrible gauntlet of lead.

Meanwhile Wolf's children busily filled their baskets as fast as they could with the dead and dying birds. Lugging the baskets to their dooryard and running back to the killing field, they soon built up rows of dead pigeons in mounds, while their mother and some of the older children began sorting and dressing the birds. Suddenly Wolf would cry out "Come, children, let's go to breakfast, guess we've got our thousand." He never stopped firing until he had slain 1,000 to 1,200 pigeons and he had an uncanny ability to reckon the count.

The first spring flights were of mature birds who flew in close formations. As the season advanced the pigeons grew more wary of the fusillade that met them from the hill each morning and they spread out in their

It was hard for hunters to miss with a sky full of pigeons.

flight patterns. But when the squabs first learned to fly the slaughter reached almost unbelievable proportions. The inexperienced birds flew low over the terrain and when fired upon huddled together in a dense flock which made it all the easier to hit dozens with each shotgun blast. Wilson remembered seeing the young birds become so confused at the murderous onslaught of lead which met them as they reached the brow of the hill that they turned back and exposed themselves a second time to the entire gamut of hunters. Few survived that double dash of death.

The pigeons flew so low that shotgun pellets were not their only fear. Some hunters found a choice spot where they could bat the birds down with clubs. Women, boys and girls frequently knocked them out of the air by throwing stones and whirling sticks into the flocks. The Wolf's house dog enjoyed leaping into the air and grabbing birds on the wing.

The excitement of the July morning's kill of a thousand or more birds over and breakfast finished, the entire Wolf family turned to processing the pigeons. It was a task that consumed the biggest share of their time during pigeon season, which began in spring and extended through early July.

First, the birds were sorted to eliminate those that had been too badly mutilated by the shotgun blast. The remainder were strung by the legs into bundles of one dozen each or salted down and packed in barrels. In season the wholesale price of fresh birds averaged ten cents per dozen but might fall to as low as five cents when the market was saturated. The barreled birds sold for less.

As the railroad had yet to reach Leelanau County, all shipments to the Chicago and eastern markets were made by lake vessel. During the height of the season scores of passenger ships and freighters stopped daily at Northport and the other ports along Lake Michigan's east coast to fill their holds with passenger pigeons.

In the Wolf household those birds not purchased by buyers for the Chicago market or hawked to ship's cooks were salted down in pork barrels for winter use. And throughout the season fresh pigeons formed a staple at most meals. The family of 14 sometimes consumed four dozen birds daily. Wilson described how they were prepared:

Ordinarily we stewed or baked the birds adding quite a large piece of salt pork to the old birds since they were never very fat. Mother had a big pot and into it she would pack as many birds as it would hold, cover them with cold water, add the pork cut into small pieces and sliced potatoes, season with salt and black pepper and stew for about forty-five minutes. Or she would place a similar combination in a big dripping pan and bake in the huge elevated oven, which was capacious enough to cook a meal for our big family.
Young birds were so enormously fat that we usually broiled or fried them, but it was a long task to prepare enough birds in this way for so many persons. Less time was required to cook young birds, they were extremely tender, but I never ate a pigeon of any age that was not delicate and delicious. The meat is darker than the dark meat of a chicken and is entirely without strong taste. When stewed the meat separates readily from the small bones and every part of the cooked bird may be eaten.

There were numerous other methods of cooking pigeons. Most nineteenth century cook books contained several recipes for cooking the wild pigeons. *The Home Messenger Book of Tested Recipes* published by a group of Detroit temperance advocates in 1878 contains a typical example:

186

A Nice Way to Cook Pigeons
Stuff the birds with a rich bread dressing; place compactly in an iron or earthen dish; season with salt, pepper and butter (or if you like best thin slices of salt pork over the top), dredge thickly with flour and nearly cover them with water. Then put over a closely fitting plate or cover, and place in a moderate oven from two to four or even five hours according to the age of the birds. If the birds are old and tough this is the best way they can be cooked as they may be made perfectly tender and much sweeter than by any other process. If the gravy is insufficient add a little water before dishing .

Another compilation of cooking lore culled from the pages of the *Detroit Free Press* in 1881 included a recipe characteristic of the times but which would be about as difficult for a modern cook to follow as it would be to obtain a passenger pigeon:

Roast Pigeons
Wipe them quite dry; truss them, and season them inside with pepper and salt, and put a piece of butter the size of a walnut in each. Put them down to a sharp fire and baste them all the time they are cooking. They will take about half an hour. Garnish them with fried parsley, and serve with a tureen of bread sauce.

The endless hours the Wolf family spent preparing pigeons for home consumption also yielded another choice commodity—feathers. The body feathers were soft and made excellent stuffing for pillows and mattresses, although they did not have the lasting qualities of goose or duck feathers. Many a neighbor was also supplied with all the feathers they wanted as well as all the birds they could eat.

Had the taking of pigeons been confined to that of residents with shotguns and Indians with long poles and blunt arrows with which they knocked the tasty squabs out of the nests, passenger pigeons flocks would undoubtedly still darken Michigan skies. But as so often has happened in American history, man's greed raised its ugly head.

While one set of entrepreneurs armed with axes and cross-cut saws attacked Michigan's seemingly limitless stands of white pine—green gold as they called them—others saw gold in the avian bounty. Rare is the Michigan local history chronicle that does not contain boasting references to the easy money made in the passenger pigeon trade. Most laments for the disappearance of the wild pigeons, in fact, seem to relate to the loss of such a lucrative opportunity.

Unrelenting warfare against the wild pigeons occurred whenever settlers and Indians discovered their immense roosting grounds or flights of the flocks blackened the skies. The huge nestings in Michigan tended to follow a biennial cycle geared to the production of beech nuts, acorns and other nuts which the pigeons relied on for food. Most of the main Michigan roosts seem to have been situated near the coasts of Lake Michigan and Lake Huron with occasional nestings on the shores of Lake Superior.

In 1858, 1864 and 1866, the pigeons established enormous roosts between South Haven and St. Joseph. Cenius H. Engle, one of the early settlers of Hartford, Van Buren County, recalled participating in a "wild pigeon chase" in 1858. The nesting extended along the lake south of South Haven, "covering many square miles where every tree was spotted with their nests." "Many times, while going out to feed," Engle wrote in an article published in the 1912 *Van Buren County History*, "they moved in such clouds that they would obscure the sun. One hearing them, not knowing the cause, would imagine a whirlwind was

An old print of a pigeon net set to capture the birds in flight.

abroad in the land."

Engle and Jacob Corwin, a 75-year-old hunter from nearby Keeler Township, determined to make some money out of the pigeons. Accordingly they set up their nets in the Hartford vicinity. Netting, the preferred method of market hunters, included varied techniques. Some pigeoners merely strung out a long fish-net like apparatus with two inch square meshes in the forest where the birds where likely to fly. On a good day hundreds of birds might become entangled in the nets.

A more sophisticated procedure involved the use of clap nets. Some trappers rigged their nets in old grain fields, baiting the area with grain or corn. Others set up their traps in the forest. After clearing the ground of underbrush the pigeoners often baited the plot with salt, which the birds craved. On each site of the salt bed a net about six feet wide by 20 to 30 feet long was secured to powerful spring poles or bent over saplings. The flutterings of one or more blinded "stool pigeons" fastened to a device that was raised up and down lured passing pigeons to the trap. The operator watched from a nearby blind until the bed was covered with the azure backs of the pigeons pecking in the soil and then yanked a lanyard which sprung the clap net.

Extremely quick and wary, at least half of the birds usually escaped the trap. But a good catch might yield as many as 1,300 birds struggling in the meshes of the net—in some cases almost lifting the entire apparatus with their combined efforts to fly.

But once in the net they were doomed. The pigeoners circled the net and every time a pigeon stuck his head through deftly nipped its neck with a pair of blacksmith's pincers, killing the birds instantly. When all were dead and the bodies piled up at a distance from the bed, the trap was reset for the next flock. Some professionals caught 5,000 birds a day using one net.

After Engle and Corwin had netted more than 12,000 birds near Hartford, they noticed the flocks were changing their flight paths to the north. Concluding that the baby birds must be nearly ready to leave their nests, they determined to acquire a quantity of those choice "butterball squabs."

After loading barrels of ice on a large wagon pulled by an ox team, the pigeoners cut their way through the forest in a northwesterly direction until they came upon a band of Potawatomi camped at the southern edge of the nesting grounds in Covert Township. There they encountered Kek-Kek, a Potawatomi who understood English. He showed them around the camp. They saw long racks of poles and bark on which were spread thousands of squabs being smoked over slow fires and numerous bushel-basket sized bark mococks full of the young birds already cured for future use.

"Are they good eating?" Engle asked Kek-Kek. Nodding his head vigorously, he exclaimed, "Num! Num! Num! It be gooder than white man's doves." Engle sampled a smoked squab as well as some johnny cake smeared with squab butter, both of which he found delicious.

The white men soon struck a bargain with the Indians, offering them one penny for each fresh squab they delivered. The entire band of Indians set off with a whoop and returned less than two hours later, each with a back pack of me-me-og, their name for the wild pigeons. Engle paid the Indians for over 2,500 squabs, which completely filled the wagon. The pigeon entrepreneurs shipped the lot to Boston and New York where they sold for $1.50 dozen, which after deducting the freight charge made the pair of pigeoners a 1,000% profit on their investment

Engle and his associate did even better in later years. He boasted that during one nesting in the

1860s nearly 15 million birds were shipped from Hartford over a 30 day period.

While nesting, the adult birds ranged for many miles in quest of acorns, beechnuts, seeds of various conifers and insects which made up their diet. Ben O. Bush, a long time employee of Kalamazoo's Globe Casket Company, remembered that when the pigeons were nesting near South Haven; "the birds used to fly over this town (Kalamazoo) every day in their quest for food, some of them going fully 75 miles in an air line from their nesting." He recalled that the sky was darkened with male birds on one day and females the next as each alternately stayed with the nest.

Needless to say, when the flocks passed over urban areas, townspeople quickly grabbed their firearms and a fusillade of potshots greeted the birds. In his *History of Benton Harbor,* published in 1915, James Pender remembered what happened when the pigeons flew over that city a half century before:

> The birds generally came from a westerly direction. These flocks were so large at times that they almost eclipsed the sun. Similar to a vast army in the air they moved in large divisions, all converging on some point in the beech woods. During the flight over Benton Harbor they were fired on from every convenient position. The slaughter of these birds was tremendous. They made excellent potpies. Every person in town or country had a share of wild bird shooting or eating.

Despite their overwhelming desire to convert the birds into potpies or cash, those who witnessed the flights of the flock frequently rhapsodized their grandeur and beauty. In 1915, Pender recalled what by then had long been a thing of the past:

> A column six or eight miles long would suddenly

appear, coming from the direction of the woods west and south of St. Joseph, and flying towards the forest east of Benton Harbor. The leaders of this great body would sometimes vary their course until it formed a large bend of more than a mile in diameter, those behind tracing the exact course of their predecessors. This would continue long after both extremities were beyond the reach of sight, so that the whole flock, with its glittering undulation, marked a space in the upper air resembling the winding of a vast river. When this bend became very great, the birds, as if sensible of the unnecessary circuitous course they were taking, suddenly changed their direction, so that what was a column before became an immense front, straightening all it crook lines until it swept the heavens in one vast extended line. Sometimes a hawk would make a sweep on a particular part of the column from a great height, when almost as quick as lightning, that part of the mass of birds shot downward out of the common track, but soon rising again, continued advancing at the same height as before. This inflection was continue by those behind, who, on arriving at this point, dived down almost perpendicularly, to a great depth, and rising followed the exact path of those that went before.

The beauty of the flights also made an indelible impression on Ulysses P. Hedrick, who grew up in the Harbor Springs area during the 1870s and 1880s. Six decades later, after he had carved out a career as a renowned horticulturist, he remembered in his book about the days of his youth, *The Land of the Crooked Tree*, that: "Black was the prevailing color in the thick cloud of birds, but at times, depending on sunlight or shadow, the number of strata, the height, or the angle of flight, the color was grayish white, a

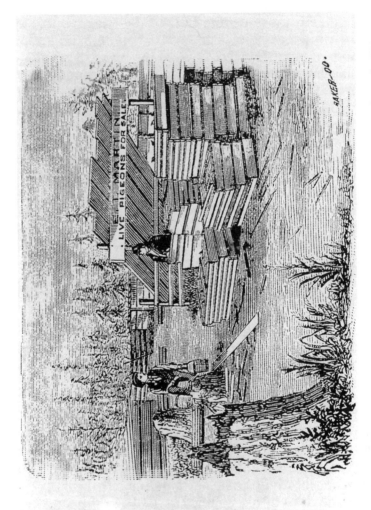

E. T. Martin's headquarters at Boyne Falls during the great pigeon slaughter of 1878.

shimmering azure, or a rich deep purple."

The beauty of the flocks in flight contrasted with another of Hedrick's childhood memories—the grisly scenes of slaughter at a pigeon roost in the woods. He described the stench of dead birds, rotten eggs and bird droppings and the din of millions of bird voices over which one could speak to another only by shouting. Amidst that bird hell Indian men chopped down trees loaded with nests, or with long poles poked the baby birds out of nests while their women and children grabbed the squabs, deftly yanked off their heads and threw their quivering bodies into great bloody heaps.

Far worse were the scenes of carnage at the periphery of the roosts where white pigeoners had rigged their clap nets. At one such trap Hedrick watched in horror as a one armed Civil War veteran named "Old Joe," his beard dripping with blood, kill as efficiently as his two-handed companions by crushing the birds' heads between his teeth.

Not all birds taken in the nets met their fate so quickly. Thousands were shipped to market alive in coops. William L. Case of Benzonia recalled earning his first real money as a youth 50 years before by working for the pigeon trappers who rushed to the Betsie River Valley during an immense roosting in 1874. Day after long day he drove a yoke of oxen hitched to a two wheeled cart, loaded again and again with live pigeons, from the nesting grounds to the saw mill where his father and brothers constructed wooden coops as fast as they could. He remembered that every team in the community, that could be spared, hauled the catch to Frankfurt where it was shipped by boat to Chicago and eastern markets. One steamer alone, that season, transported a shipment of some 36,000 live pigeons to a sporting club in Oswego, N.Y.

Trapshooting, before "clay pigeons" had been

substituted for the real thing, took a heavy toll of passenger pigeons. Throughout the nineteenth century, when a sportsman yelled "pull," a live pigeon was released. A successful shot brought down the bird, followed by a flutter of feathers and the clapping of spectators. In 1869, a single marksman in Chicago killed 605 birds in about seven hours, knocking down more than 80% of the birds released. In 1881, members of the New York Association for the Protection of Fish and Game blasted 20,000 wild pigeons at a gala trap shoot on Coney Island. Another trapshooting promoter boasted that he had killed more than 27,000 birds alone during his heyday.

Despite the unrelenting warfare levied against the wild pigeons, young and old, for food, profit and sport, the birds continued to roost in seemingly unparalleled numbers. In 1874 and 1876, pigeoners exploited enormous nestings near Shelby, Oceana County. In 1874, the shipments of dead birds alone from Shelby averaged 100 barrels, each containing approximately 500 birds, per day for more than 30 days—in excess of 1.5 million birds.

The largest recorded roosting in Michigan came in 1878. Three to ten miles wide, it stretched for 40 miles in the beech forest east of Petoskey. Another nesting about half that large was located near Boyne Falls. Farther south, on the Manistee River, the pigeons established a roost encompassing 130 square miles.

From all directions an itinerant army of pigeoners estimated at 2,000 strong made a bee line for Petoskey and pitched in to produce an epic slaughter. Before they were done that season, counting the dead and dying birds left in the woods and the squabs that starved in the nest after their parents were netted, an estimated one billion pigeons "had been sacrificed to mammon!"

Worse yet, what happened to the flock in Michigan was but part of its odyssey of death that year. Prior to roosting in Petoskey, the birds had nested in Missouri in April, where the squabs had been similarly butchered by market hunters. Those pigeoners had followed the flights to Petoskey and when the flock left Michigan and flew eastward, the hunters learned via telegrams sent to all locales where they were likely to nest a third time that the birds had settled in the Catskill Mountains of New York. The insatiable pigeoners soon arrived to resume their butchery anew.

It was too much! The pigeons evidently required a large breeding population to restore the birds who died via natural predators and periodic calamities like ice storms which sometimes decimated flocks. Once their numbers dropped below that level they were doomed as a species.

The 1878 Petoskey holocaust was the last roosting of commercial significance in Michigan. The flocks were never seen after that in the Northport vicinity. Two years later they came to Benzie County for the last time. In 1881, however, they established another great roost near Petoskey. They built their nests and laid their eggs late in April. Before the pigeoners could begin their cruel work, nature mercifully interceded. Case, the Benzonia youth who had hauled so many live pigeons to market, quoted an eyewitness account of what happened:

A big wind and storm of sleet came up just at dusk and the birds left. There was a heavy fog on Lake Michigan and the birds were swallowed up in the storm. Anyhow, they disappeared then and there. I have heard tell of the beach being strewn for miles with dead pigeons, and I heard an old woodsman tell of the stench arising from the dead pigeons in the woods.

Etta Wilson remembered a similar mysterious

tragedy occurring about that same time at Northport:

> One day in early summer we got up in the morning to find Grand Traverse Bay covered with dead pigeons and the shore strewn with their bodies where the undulating back wash of the night had brought them in from the big lake. The night had been quiet. There had been no storm and no fog...Later in the day the merciful wind came up from southwest and carried back to the bosom of the big lake the vast and silent caravan of gently birds whose very attractiveness and usefulness had led to their extinction.
> Denied a foothold on the earth which was made for all creatures, without one safe spot on which they might rest, homes destroyed, their young killed, harassed and tormented on every side, had they in desperation flown themselves into the waters of oblivion?

When the Indians of nearby Peshabetown saw the windrows of dead birds on the beach, they said: "They have committed suicide. Their persecution was more than any living being could endure."

Scattered sightings of small flocks continued to be reported over the following two decades. In 1886, a little flock of about 600 pairs was discovered nesting in a swamp near Lake City, Missaukee County. That would be the last known time when more than two or three pairs were found nesting together. Two years later, a flock of about 200 was spotted near Vicksburg, Kalamazoo County.

In 1888, ornithologist William Brewster spent several weeks in northern Michigan in hopes of studying a large nesting. He learned that several thousand wild pigeons had appeared in April of that year near Cadillac, and that all the local pigeoners had gotten their gear together in high hope of another

Jacob Studer's *Birds of North America* published in 1888 included a
lithograph of passenger pigeons. By then they were a dying species.

"killing." The flock was traced as far north as Oden, Emmit County, where, much to the chagrin of the hunters, it disappeared.

After 1888, no large flocks of passenger pigeons were reported anywhere. The sightings of single individuals began to be noted in scientific journals. In 1895 Chief Pokagon published an article about the pigeons in which he lamented:

> We strain our eyes in Spring and Autumn in vain to catch a glimpse of these pilgrims. White men tell us they have moved in a body to the Rocky Mountain region, where they are as plentiful as they were here, but when we ask red men, who are familiar with the mountain country, about them, they shake their heads in disbelief.

In 1897, a "day late and a dollar short," the Michigan legislature passed a law prohibiting the killing of passenger pigeons at any time of year, for a period of ten years. On September 14, 1898, a Detroit sportsman named P. E. Moody shot the last confirmed specimen in the wild, an immature bird, near Delroy, Wayne County. He proudly had it mounted by a renowned Detroit taxidermist and sold it to a Canadian collector.

That left only Martha, and a handful of other captive passenger pigeons. Martha, probably the offspring of a pair of birds captured in Wisconsin, had arrived at the Cincinnati Zoological Garden sometime prior to 1902. Three years after that date, the Michigan legislature removed the passenger pigeon from the class of game birds, making illegal its killing at any time of the year—if one could be found that is.

The Cincinnati Zoo issued a standing offer of $1000, equal to at least 20 times that amount in current dollars, for a mate to breed with Martha. Bounty hunters ransacked the wilds of the Rocky

Mountains and the backwoods of Canada to no avail. Meanwhile school children across the country made pilgrimages to Cincinnati to tiptoe by Martha's cage. Then at 1 p.m. on September 1, 1914, surrounded by a hushed gathering of distinguished ornithologists, Martha fell to the floor of her cage and lay stiff and cold. The last of her species, she was an estimated 29-years-old when she died. Her mounted body resides in the Smithsonian Institute.

Like so many of the wild things that once roamed unfettered—great herds of shaggy buffalo, cagey wolf packs, beautiful Michigan graylings, aboriginal tribesmen—apparently the continent was not big enough for them and civilization too. Whether there is room enough in the continent for whooping cranes, spotted owls, piping plovers and other endangered species remains to be determined.

Martha, the last passenger pigeon on the earth.

From Gutter to Pulpit: Battling Demon Rum in Michigan

Henry O. Wills, the "whiskey voiced" evangelist, delivered temperance
lectures to Detroiters from atop his buggy.

Clad in a black suit and derby, the muscular, middle-aged man sporting a thick, droopy mustache personified John L. Sullivan or one of the other hard drinking, hard-hitting Irish prize fighters who enlivened ring history during the glory days of bare knuckle bouts. He pulled his buggy to a stop before the Civil War Soldier's Monument at the intersection of Woodward Ave. and Campus Martius in downtown Detroit, climbed into the back, raised a banner on a staff and began singing in a harsh "whiskey voice" the old revival hymn "Come to Jesus."

It was an early evening in the summer of 1883 and the streets bustled with workers making their way home. Within minutes a crowd had surrounded the buggy to stare at the incongruous spectacle. Then the burley singer ended his hymn and began to address the crowd in his raspy voice: "For 46 years I was a thief, a liar, and a drunkard. I couldn't say 50 words without 45 of em' being oaths and lies. But at last a great change came over me. O' I can't begin to tell what a glad day that was when I experienced religion. The old Henry O. Wills died and a new man took his place. Thank God, old Wills is dead!"

Wills preached his hoarse message across Michigan throughout the 1880s, and he also told the story of his dastardly past life in a volume published in 1890, *Twice Born, or the Two Lives of Henry O. Wills, Evangelist.* Therein he described his remarkable careers as "wharf-rat, sneak thief, convict, soldier, bounty jumper, fakir, fireman, ward-heeler, and a plug-ugly." The latter, incidently, was a member of a gang of New York City Irish toughs who wore enormous plug, or top, hats which they stuffed with wool and leather and pulled down over their ears to serve as helmets when they went into battle.

Wills' colorful confessions comprised but one of numerous volumes written by low-down drunks,

203

gamblers and sundry other profligates who rose from the gutter to the pulpit during the 19th century. Having a book to hawk following a rousing bible thumping seemed to lend a sense of legitimacy to the proceedings. Many of the born-again literati boasted of wicked forays into Michigan. Others wrote of evangelical campaigns conducted in the cities and towns of the Wolverine State after they had renounced their naughty ways. Whether they succeeded in upgrading the morals of Michigan citizens or merely made a better living via the collection plate is open to conjecture. One thing is certain, their books make fascinating reading, particularly the exploits prior to "seeing the light."

John Gough, probably the first "tosspot" to make a career out of publicly describing his intemperate behavior, ventured into Michigan as early as 1850. Born in 1817 in England, Gough immigrated to New York City at the age of 12. He began drinking in earnest when he reached 18 and, as outlined in his autobiography, the following seven years were little more than one protracted binge. He and his drinking buddies were great jokesters while under the influence. One day in 1842, for example, they wandered into a Methodist church where services were being held by a congregation of Millerites. Followers of William Miller, who prophesied the exact date the world would end, the Millerites were prepared to soon ascend directly to Heaven. Gough and his buddies began passing a half-filled spittoon down the pews, announcing they were taking a collection for ascension robes for the needy.

Not long after that episode Gough drank himself out of a job and home. Staggering along the streets of Worchester, Massachusetts, "a wretched, shabby looking drunkard, a living, walking disgrace," he met a kind stranger who convinced him to sign the pledge of total abstinence. Although he suffered a severe

John Gough's autobiography included this print of a street preacher and his audience.

bout of withdrawal sickness, Gough stuck with the pledge and before long had launched a career lecturing to others about temperance. He spoke 386 times during his first year alone. Collection plates passed around after his descriptions of the disgusting drunkard's life he had renounced brought him more money than he had ever made before.

During Gough's foray into Michigan in 1850 he succeeded in convincing no less than 2,446 Detroit residents to sign the pledge. Since that number represented one out of every ten men, women and children who lived in the city then, Detroit must have been a rum seller's paradise prior to Gough's onslaught. Bouyed by such phenomenal success, Gough conducted additional campaigns across Michigan, as well, in particular while visiting friends in Adrian and Galesburg. During 17 years of temperance lectures, Gough addressed some 5,000 audiences in America and Europe. His oratorical ability netted him "a moderate fortune" prior to his death in 1886.

Another early soak-turned-speaker, George M. Dutcher, was somewhat of a protege of Gough's, having been given a $20 bill by that worthy which helped him over a dry spell during the beginnings of his pulpit career. Dutcher, as detailed in his 1872 autobiography, *Disenthralled: A Story of My Life,* blamed his alcoholism on the early influence of his parents, a set of sots from New York's Catskill Mountains. Taunted by fellow pupils as "the son of a drunkard," Dutcher quit school at the age of ten and went to work for a neighboring farmer, an employer who drank hard throughout the day and didn't like to drink alone. Soon his young farm hand was pounding down the potations with the best of them. Thus Dutcher and his youthful companions were "led on, step by step, gradually, not only in rum-drinking, but in card playing and Sabbath breaking, until vice so completely overmastered them that, even in boyhood,

206

they were beginning to enter the broad road which winds down to the gates of hell."

Contrary to the majority of the literary ex-guzzlers, who alloted plenty of pages to moralizing, Dutcher devoted nine tenths of his 276 page reminiscences to his tipsy journey down that broad road. Perhaps, that is why his book is more readable than most of the ilk. Ultimately, however, following a particularly grand spree which brought on the delirium tremors Dutcher saw the light, signed a pledge and took the story of his ne'er-do-well life on the road.

The year 1868 found Dutcher campaigning for temperance in Michigan. He lectured in Detroit, Mount Clemens, St. Clair, Saginaw, Bay City, Ann Arbor, Battle Creek and elsewhere. The collection plate allowed him a comfortable living at the expense of others. Following one of his Michigan lectures, for example, a "poor drunkard" told him of his misery and degradation then said: "There is a dollar; the only one I have in the world, and I want you to take it and let me sign the pledge." Dutcher had no choice but to take the man's last dollar for the good that he thought it would do him.

Then there was Mason Long "the converted gambler." Long originally hailed from Ohio where he had experienced a miserable childhood. Orphaned at the age of ten, he was bound out to a wealthy German farmer in Medina County, Ohio, who worked him like a slave until he was 18. In the spring of 1862, Long enlisted with the 112th Illinois Infantry to save the Union. Like many another recruit he learned to while away long hours in camp by gambling. He became adept at casino, poker, chuck-a-luck and other games of chance and he soon made those games less a matter of chance for himself through a variety of "tricks" including marked cards, dealing from the bottom of the deck and the old ace up the sleeve. Long won thousands of dollars from fellow soldiers and squandered most of it as fast as he could.

Following his discharge in 1865, Long moved to Fort Wayne, Indiana, where he invested the $2,800 left of his gambling spoils in a grocery business. It was in Fort Wayne that he picked up his second vice-tippling. It began, so his 1878 autobiography stated, when a local doctor prescribed whiskey as a tonic for his bad heart. He started by taking it by the spoonful and found it so stimulating that within three months he was quaffing it freely out of a gallon jug.

Under the sway of his twin vices, Long deserted his legitimate grocery business and became a professional gambler. He started as a faro dealer in a local gaming house then gravitated to lotteries, horse racing and other forms of gambling. For years Long toured all the trotting races on the Indiana and Michigan circuits. In his memoirs, he recalled visiting the famous race course at Jackson many times, invariably losing large sums.

At Jackson in 1872, his dissipation began to catch up with him. Suffering from the effects of whiskey and the heat, he succumbed to a sunstroke and crumpled to the ground. Carried from the racing park to the Union Hotel, he remained unconscious for several days and did not recover completely for months.

Jackson proved a bad luck city for Long. In 1876 he again followed the racing circuit to Jackson where he promptly lost every penny he had in a faro game. Leaving his luggage in lieu of payment for his hotel bill, Long skipped town on the horse train headed for Saginaw. Borrowing a dollar from a crony, he purchased a cheap cardboard valise and trudged in the rain to a hotel, expecting to get a room on the strength of his new luggage. The landlord took one look at his satchel, which the rain had caused to disintegrate, revealing its sole contents—one pair of dirty socks—and announced: "We're all full." Long

Mason Long's first appearance at Fort Wayne, Indiana, drew a huge crowd of sinners.

glanced down at his ruined valise, dropped it on the spot and retreated amidst a roar of laughter from the crowd which filled the lobby.

Down but not out, the gambler managed to borrow a small stake and in a short time had relieved some Saginaw citizens of $550 in a faro game and he was soon off for Detroit in high style.

In 1877, Long visited a temperance meeting out of curiosity and promptly got converted. Before long he joined the ranks of those ex-sinners able to parley their new-found salvation into a pulpit career. The following year found Long engaged in a crusade in Michigan which included a very successful campaign against the souses of Ann Arbor. In addition to his autobiographical tome, Long also authored the volumes *Save the Girls* and *Fallen Women,* lengthy treatises exposing the evils of prostitution and white slavery, the intimate workings of which the converted gambler seemed to know a good deal more about than a preacher should have.

Mason's autobiography does not record whether he ever tried out his pulpit antics in his old Michigan nemesis—Jackson. Perhaps he retained enough of the gambler's savvy to not push his luck too far. Other of his professional kindred, however, did periodically conduct crusades in what was "called the hardest city in Michigan."

In the fall of 1883, the Rev. Joseph H. Weber, a Methodist evangelist who specialized in "revival tornadoes," roared into Jackson. While "Satan had become so entrenched as to defy all that was good," Weber blew "old Nick" away in a series of revival meetings that netted 800 converts. Weber's success came in part, according to the biographical volume he authorized a fellow minister, the Rev. Martin Wells Knapp, to produce, from his ability to look sinners straight in the eye and know full well what they were up to. For, he, Weber, had been a very naughty man prior to conversion.

Weber, it seems, had started life with the deck stacked against him. His parents were Catholics, enslaved to what he saw in retrospect as "Romish superstitions." His father, a German who liked his beer a bit too much, set a poor example. Young Weber quit school to take his first job as a bartender in a Cincinnati tavern. He was so short that the owner had to erect a rack behind the bar for him to stand on to serve patrons. There, Weber's natural propensity for spirituous beverages was further strengthened.

If that were not enough to send him on the path to perdition, he developed a fondness for "theatricals." He organized a minstrel troupe and became adept at jigging and clogging. Next he bought a violin and soon grew proficient enough to play at dances. Little did he know then that he would later thunder from the pulpit: "The dance-house, the rink, the saloon, the circus, and the theatre are Satan's churches."

Soon Weber found himself "young in years, but old in vice. Quaffing iniquity as if it were some delicious nectar, and loving the deadly draught." Fortunately, just as he dangled on the brink of a "Niagara of sin and dissipation," he was befriended by a street evangelist who introduced him to the local YMCA. It was not long before he had renounced his evil ways and launched his own career as Rev. Joseph Weber,Evangelist, "the converted Roman Catholic."

In 1887, while en route for a soul-saving tour of California the evangelical tornado was urgently called to Marcellus, Michigan where, apparently, too many citizens were getting "three sheets to the wind." He spent much of the following year engaged in a revival cyclone in southern Michigan, ripping through White Pigeon, Bronson, Coldwater, Leslie, Quincy, Nottawa, Union City, Hillsdale and Adrian where Weber fought to break citizens' "bondage to the card table, rink, dance hall open and the other sinful amusements,"

211

which he had known so well before his conversion.

While Michigan apparently proved fertile ground for Weber's ministries, it nearly brought the downfall of another Buckeye evangelist, Samuel W. Shockey, author of an 1892 autobiography, *Twenty-five Years Fighting Fate*.... Born in 1858 in Hardin County, Ohio, Shockey developed to wanderlust at the age of nine, and ran away from home and got a job with a traveling side show. Over the course of the following nine years he worked as a farm hand, hawked books door to door and peddled glass and tinware across the midwestern states. Somehow he managed to resist the temptations of drink, tobacco and other iniquities. Spring 1878 found him attending the university at Ada, Ohio. One day he wandered into a Methodist revival meeting held across the street from his room. Typically, almost before he could shout "Praise the Lord!" he had become an evangelist himself.

Shockey's new career went well at first as he traveled throughout Ohio conducting rousing revivals. He married in 1879 with the understanding that he and his wife would soon embark on a missionary tour of India. She reneged on the agreement, however, and refused to participate in any of his evangelistic tomfoolery. Shortly after the birth of his baby daughter, Shockey rambled off to Canada on an evangelical tour. When he returned to the states, he found that his wife had started divorce proceedings. She won the divorce, as well as an alimony settlement of $1,300, a hefty sum at a time when the average factory worker considered himself lucky to earn $1.25 for a ten-hour work day.

Distraught over his turn of fortune and faced with the task of raising the $1,300, Shocky somehow wound up in Manistee, Michigan. He secured a position teaching in a one room country school near Bear Lake, 15 miles to the north. Shockey nearly made it through the term, but overwhelmed by his woes, he began downing the Devil's potion right in the classroom! He began with a little wine for his stomach's sake. Then it was whiskey, followed by a gallon of pure alcohol, which was soon gone. His Bear Lake neighbors told him if he continued drinking he would soon kill himself.

Things soon got worse. He left for Ohio on a business tour and was arrested for absconding with several hundred dollars of his landlady's cash. Extradited to Michigan and lodged in jail, he succeeded in beating that rap, but the shame of it all cut deeply.

Shockey took a job as tallyman on the Manistee lumber boats for a while, then shipped out for Wisconsin. There, he launched a new career as a phrenologist, a practitioner of the science of ascertaining character by reading the bumps on a subjects head. His phrenology lectures and demonstrations went well until he began guzzling again. Following a particularly memorable jag in company with a reunion of Masons in St. Paul, Minnesota, following which Shockey woke up in the mud "busted flat," he chanced to come across a gypsy camp.

The gypsies hospitably welcomed the muddy drunk into their fold and while traveling with them he learned the art of fortune telling. Before long, Shockey branched out on his own, telling fortunes in taverns. Leaving the gypsies, he parleyed his double-barreled approach to separating the suckers from their stash by reading their heads and their palms, into a lucrative career.

Shockey traveled out west where he became a cowboy for a spell, then joined the cavalry and deserted. No matter how much money he made, he spent it all in saloons. He computed that in his various travels he had lost no less than ten valises by getting drunk and forgetting them. By 1890 Shockey's

George Dutcher's spirited autobiography featured an illustration of a spree in a Chicago grog shop.

alcoholism had reached the point where he "had to have four or five glasses of whiskey before I could eat my breakfast."

Then came the "jim-jams" and delirium tremors. In Grand Rapids, Michigan, that year he got spifflicated, creating such a spectacle on the street that a crowd gathered to watch his antics. The local authorities let him sleep that jag off in the city lock-up.

Finally, after ten years as a toper, Shockey "found Jesus" again and gave up his low-down ways. He ended his autobiography published in 1892 with the statement that he had "not taken a drop of intoxicating drink" since Thanksgiving, 1891. We can only hope that he succeeded in staying on the wagon as he hawked his book during the remainder of his career as a triple threat temperance crusader—combining preaching, phrenology and fortune telling.

Then there was that distinctive division of temperance lecturers whose life prior to the pulpit had coupled prize fighting with pouring down the potables. Joseph F. Hess, "the converted prize fighter and saloon-keeper," told his sad story in *Out of Darkness Into Light*... published in 1890. Born in Buffalo, N.Y., in 1851, of German parentage, Hess began his working life in a brickyard at the age of 11. His initial foray into sin came not through tobacco or rum but via the Devil disguised as a sweet roll.

It seems that there was a bakery in Buffalo that made sweet rolls so delicious that as he passed by young Hess found them irresistible. So he set up a charge account there in his father's name and proceeded to enjoy prodigious quantities of the sticky buns, that is, until the baker sought to settle the bill with his father. At that point Hess found it advisable to leave home in a hurry. He shipped aboard the propeller *Burlington* as a deckhand. By the time the ship reached Detroit Hess and a chum had decided they were ill suited to "a life on the lake wave." The two jumped ship and spent the next 24 hours hiding beneath a wooden sidewalk until the vessel left the city. Hess had plenty of time during that period to contemplate the delicious sweet rolls that had landed him in that fix.

From Detroit the boys headed south, working and begging along the way, until at Nashville, Tennessee, they found "the air heavily laden with the fumes of powder" from Union and Confederate cannons and they wisely retreated back to Buffalo. Hess stayed at home for awhile, but apparently his sticky bun adventure had implanted in him "a spirit of unrest and dissatisfaction." His father sought to quell those urges by apprenticing him to a local cooper, but Hess found barrel making not to his liking, either. What's more he soon "got in with evil companions, and became one of that much-to-be despised class, street corner loafers."

One of his fellow loafers invited Hess to a party. There, a pretty girl offered him a glass of wine. When he refused, telling her he had vowed to his parents never to touch strong drink, she ridiculed him as a mama's boy. Hess yielded to the temptress, took his first glass of wine at the age of 15 and thus begun his lengthy "battles with the demon alcohol, the first gun of misery, degradation and sin having been fired by that young lady."

Hess soon "became reckless and rapidly gave up to a life of dissipation, spending the day in toil and the night in empty pleasures, thus unfitting himself for the day's labor." Fired from his job as a result of his nightly carousing, Hess against tried his luck as a sailor. But as his steamer passed up the Detroit River it collided with another vessel and sank. Hess narrowly escaped drowning in the ice laden water by swimming to the Canadian shore. Taken to Detroit, he received his pay from the owner of the unfortunate vessel, bought himself a new suit of clothes and caught the next train for Toledo. The first structure he saw after leaving the depot was a pub. Entering it, he woke up the next morning behind bars, broke and dressed in a ragged old suit which someone had swapped for his new one as he lay dead drunk in an alley. A Toledo judge sentenced him to 60 days in jail on the charge of drunk and disorderly conduct.

Following his release, Hess got a construction job on the levee in Toledo. There he first began to learn the "manly art." Armed with his new skill, Hess left Toledo to wander about the country for several years stopping wherever he could secure a prize fight. But as more and more of his opponents hit the canvas, Hess hit the bottle with increasing frequency.

His bouts with booze netted him several more jail terms, as well. Following a 90 day sentence for cleaning out a Chicago saloon, of its occupants, that is, Hess decided to clean out his own system through a season as a lumberjack in the Michigan woods. He left the lumber camp with his own hard earned wages as well as the greater part of the other shanty boys' pay taken at the card table.

Soon Hess was back at his old habits, trading punches for money and blowing every cent he made on wild sprees. At Grand Rapids in 1882, Hess knocked out Thomas Kanear in four rounds. Two years later he stepped into the wrestling ring with "Primrose, the champion collar and elbow wrestler of Michigan." The match lasted two hours, ending with a victory for Hess and the $500 prize.

Eventually, Hess settled down in Rochester, N.Y., where he operated a tavern and gambling hall. Being the proprietor of his own bar made it all the easier for him to drink to excess. By 1885, he had begun having bouts with that ogre of all the literary dipsomaniacs, the delirium tremens. Shortly after the snakes and shakes began he wisely took the pledge at

217

A typical scene from John Gough's life before he "saw the light".

a temperance meeting and, as was the fashion, began his own career as a pulpit reformer and book vendor. Needless to say, his autobiography lost much of its vim and vigor following his transformation.

The memoirs of another pugilist, *The Life and Adventures of Ben Hogan, The Wickedest Man in the World,* retained its punch right through the final chapter largely because its author, George Francis Trainer, who wrote the 1878 volume based on Hogan's oral testimony left a good deal of doubt as to whether its hero actually had renounced his wicked ways. Hogan, whose real name was Hagan, emigrated as a young boy with his family from Germany to New York in 1852. His life on the shady side began shortly thereafter when he broke into a minister's house, stole a number of valuable books containing fine engravings, tore out the pictures, threw away the books, and exhibited the prints in a gallery, charging two cents admission. It did not take the long arm of the law long to collar the young biblioclast and a judge meted him a well deserved 30 day stint in the penitentiary.

A similar offense landed Hogan in the Rochester, N.Y., Reform School for 90 days. Hogan testified in his book that "he learned nothing good during his sojourn there." What he had learned, however ,was to use his dukes rather well. Supplementing that proficiency with boxing lessons in a New York gymnasium, Hogan took the ring name "The Sailor Boy," and began touring the country, earning his living via his fists, gambling and assorted con-games.

In 1861, he shot to death three rival gamblers in Mobile, Alabama. During the Civil War he served as a spy in both the Union and Confederate armies and also made additional money as a bounty jumper. Finding himself in Louisville, Kentucky ,when the war ended, Hogan made a quick $20,000 by cheating the members of a Black regiment out of their mustering out pay. He generously changed their large bills into smaller bills that were actually advertisements which resembled green backs.

Those exploits proved small potatoes for what Hogan accomplished when he set up shop in the tough Pennsylvania oil country renowned for such legendary hell holes as Pithole and Petrolia. When he was not polishing opponents off in the ring before crowds of oil drillers, he was separating them from their paychecks in card games, bamboozling them through get-rich-quick schemes and helped them forget their hard work via his gin mills and houses of ill-repute. Not only had Hogan become a very wicked man, the pages of his autobiography seem to reflect a certain pride in his accomplishments.

When the Pennsylvania authorities began breathing down his neck, Hogan pulled up stakes, bouncing around the midwest to wherever he could find a good poker game or ring challenger. He landed in Detroit in 1875, where among other endeavors he spent six weeks training a huge fighter named McLaughlin for an upcoming match against Martin, "the butcher boy of Ypsilanti." Hogan attended boxing matches in Ypsilanti and Grand Rapids. He liked the "Furniture City" so well that he opened a gymnasium there and began delivering lectures on "Physical Culture" in the surrounding villages.

A Grand Rapids incident which Hogan told with great relish in his book also made it into the *Grand Rapids Times*. It seems the "wickedest man on earth" was standing on a Monroe Street corner one day, dressed in a black suit and high collar, with a text book on gymnastics under his arm. Mistaking him for a clergyman and his book for the Bible, a minister from a nearby town introduced himself to Hogan and asked whether the good reverend might entertain him, a hungry visitor to the metropolis, in his home. Hogan went along with the blunder as a practical joke and escorted the divine to his gymnasium where he gave him an exhibition of weight lifting and bag punching. The bewildered minister was only too happy to seek his free lunch elsewhere among more genuine brothers of the cloth.

Toward the conclusion of his autobiography, Hogan summarized the lessons on intemperance he had learned during his more than two decade long career as the wickedest man in the world: "First, absolute purity in all liquors. Second, the substitution of beer and light wines for whiskey and other strong drinks. Third, the regeneration of places where wine and beer may be obtained, so that they can be visited by anybody without the sacrifice of respectability." In essence, his philosophy was that human nature being what it is, total abstinence was an impossibility so why not try moderation.

Whether the advice of Hogan, the unrepentant rascal, had a more telling effect than that of Brothers Weber, Long, Dutcher, Hess, Gough, Wells ,Shockey and other bible thumping reformers who told about their wicked ways in autobiographies must remain a matter of personal choice. Perhaps each reformer's ultimate success was best reckoned by his bank book. Gough made enough money, for example, to construct a fashionable Italianate mansion filled with opulent furnishings in West Boyleston, Massachusetts. His hard hitting colleague, Hess, met the issue head on in his book: "I do make speeches for money... Does any man work without getting pay? Does any man sell goods simply for glory?"

Was it glory, gain or gin that motivated them to tell their intemperate stories? Were they saints, sinners or merely souses with a pen? A century and more after their autobiographies were written, it is unlikely those questions can ever be answered.

But by committing their shortcomings to the pages of a book they achieved a type of immortality denied

Ben Hogan, "the wickedest man in the world," downed nearly as many opponents as he did bottles of whiskey.

the majority of their contemporaries who stayed on the straight and narrow. And the colorful characters that emerge from those pages, whether they be rogues or raconteurs, were seldom dull. Take our raspy-voiced friend, George O. Wills, for example, who sang hymns to Detroiters from the back of his buggy. Shortly after his conversion, he entered one of his former haunts to spread the word to the tipplers. Ridiculed as a "crank" by his old cronies in a attempt to make him lose his temper and show he was not so holy, Wells roared to them between clenched teeth: "Will you please tell me what keeps my hands down by my side, or why I don't knock your nose all over your face?" That not too long after in Saginaw, he "thumped the whey out of some dirty dog on the street car" who was teasing him in a similar manner only makes his story the more believable and entertaining. A writer could do worse than to entertain his readers. Perhaps that is redeeming enough.

Michigan at the "White City": The Columbian Exposition of 1893

Detroit's Berry Brothers Co. displayed a giant red wood plank sealed with their varnish at the World's Fair.

In fourteen hundred ninety two
Columbus sailed the ocean blue

F our centuries later America commemorated Columbus's discovery of the New World with a colossal world's fair known as the Columbian Exposition. Of the thirteen international expositions that had succeeded London's 1851 Crystal Palace, the United States had hosted only the 1876 Centennial Exposition in Philadelphia. Now Americans set their sights on surpassing the 1889 Paris Exposition, which had produced the Eiffel Tower and won the world's accolades as the century's best fair. Condescending older nations might still consider the United States a raw frontier, but Americans intended to showcase their progress in fine arts, industry, technology and agriculture and "warm the world up to the blood heat of youth—to prove that there is no bottom to American speed."

Introduction of the World's Fair bill in the United States Senate brought brisk competition for the exposition's location. New York City and Chicago emerged as the leading aspirants. As New York City depreciated its upstart western rival, Chicago rolled up its sleeves, bonded $10 million, promised a satisfactory site and in 1890 won the prize. An undeveloped five-hundred-acre tract of marsh and sand dunes, located on the lakefront seven miles south of the Chicago Loop, was selected for the fair. Frederick Law Olmsted designed a plan for Jackson Park, and a force of 15,000 laborers began filling and leveling the plot, dredging canals and lagoons, and constructing enormous neoclassical structures, whose dazzling marble-like appearance produced the effect of a "white city." The country projected designs on such a massive scale that when 1892 rolled around, the grounds lay far from completion. No matter, the world would celebrate the 401st anniversary of Columbus's discovery.

As the sixteen huge *beaux arts* exhibition halls financed by the United States took shape, nineteen foreign nations constructed buildings representative of their cultures, and scores contributed samples of their natural resources and native industries. Germany sponsored the Krupp Gun exhibit featuring a 120-ton cannon, the largest gun yet manufactured; Spain sent relics of Columbus and a replica of the convent of La Rabida; Australia added a bushman's cabin and an assortment of aborigines; and Siberia displayed goods manufactured in its infamous penal colony. Thirty-nine U. S. states set up structures on the northern periphery of Jackson Park to serve as headquarters for their representatives and rest area for citizens.

The Great Lakes states interpreted Chicago's victory as a vindication of their own importance. Illinois provided a huge, domed structure that vied with the main exhibition buildings in grandeur, while Minnesota, Wisconsin, Indiana, Ohio and Michigan erected substantial buildings. "The world is coming to see us, and we must put on our good clothes," announced I. M. Weston, president of the Michigan Board of World's Fair Managers.

The Michigan State Legislature had created the Board of World's Fair Managers and appropriated $100,000 for exhibits on 21 July 1891. Governor E. B. Winans appointed board members representing the state's major geographical and economic constituencies: Grand Rapids lumberman I. M. Weston, the forest industries; Peter White of Marquette, the mineral resources; E. H. Beldon, a Jackson County farmer, the agricultural interests; J. W. Flynn, ex-president of the Detroit Board of Trade, the manufacturers; and Mrs. Julia A. Pond of Hillsdale and Mrs. J. S. Valentine of Lansing, Michigan's distaff side. Governor Winans, and in 1893 his successor,

Governor John T. Rich, served as ex officio members. Mark W. Stevens of Flint rounded out the board as secretary. The managers divided up the state and appointed representatives from each county to assist in disseminating information and collecting exhibits.

Armed with the $100,000 appropriation, which was increased by $25,000 in 1893, the board set out to show the world that "the creator might have made a better state than Michigan, but he never did." Representatives of special interest groups seeking a share of the budget soon made their pitches. Professor W. J. Beal of the Michigan Agricultural College submitted a plan for a forestry exhibit. The Rev. Jameson and Bishop Gillespie urged a religious exhibit; Henry Chamberlain from Three Oaks pushed the farmer's cause; Mrs. James Burrill Angell and Mrs. John J. Bagley promoted woman's work; and Mortimer E. Cooley advocated more for the University of Michigan. F. A. Washburn left his Belding Silk Works to campaign for manufacturers, and an entire delegation of fruit growers arrived to speak for the state's pomological interests. On 5 January 1892 President Weston reported that at least $250,000 would be needed to satisfy the demands already submitted. With no additional appropriations in sight, those who wanted a better exhibit would have to fund the excess themselves.

When the state legislature's $125,000 appropriation was divided, approximately $50,000 was allocated for exhibits. The largest share, roughly $20.000, went to the agricultural and horticultural interests. The board distributed $12,000 for the mineral exhibit; $5,500 for general state exhibits, including $676 to edit a new edition of *Michigan and Its Resources,* a 290-page promotional piece handed out at the fair; $5,000 for educational exhibits; and $4,500 for forestry exhibits. Women's work received a paltry $1,415.

Michigan's impressive World's Fair Building was constructed of
Michigan lumber for $20,000.

About one-half of the state appropriations went for constructing, furnishing and maintaining the Michigan State Building, which became the major focus of the board's efforts. While promoting Michigan's virtues, the building would serve as headquarters for state delegates and a rest area—a bit of the old home soil—where Michiganians could seek respite from the turmoil and bewilderment of the vast fairgrounds. Other states, such as Illinois and California, appropriated more extravagant sums for the exposition, but Michigan's managers planned to make up in good taste what they lacked in funds.

They immediately ran into trouble. The board drew up rough plans, allocating $20,000 for construction of the state building. Early in August 1891, President Weston arrived in Chicago to arrange for a site and get the plan approved. Weston found the plot allocated Michigan both poorly located and too small. Nothing could be done about the size, but he succeeded in negotiating a rearrangement of division lines to give Michigan a nice corner lot. Ohio's lot abutted Michigan's on the east, while Wisconsin's and Indiana's lay to the south. Up the street was California's opulent $300,000 mission-style showplace. Michigan's managers later testily prohibited the sale of "California Orange Cider" (probably orange juice) on the Michigan grounds.

When Weston submitted sketches for the Michigan Building he encountered more problems. The plans showed a three-story, 144 foot x 104 foot structure divided into large rooms and wrapped with a two-story veranda. The supervising architect objected—the building was too large for the lot; it left no lawn; and the veranda was unsightly. Weston took umbrage; Michigan was not responsible for the puny lot. It needed a large building to accommodate the many visitors expected, he argued, and since the funds allocated could not build a structure both large

229

and sightly, architectural considerations would have to be limited. Furthermore, the porch was an absolute necessity, since Michiganians "were accustomed to open air and shade in summer time, and would have it!" After prolonged bickering, Weston won. Michigan would have "a plain but large, comfortable, and convenient building constructed of wood typical of the leading lumbering state in the Union."

On 11 February 1892 the board adopted the architectural plans submitted by Mortimer L. Smith and Son of Detroit. Similar to the Indiana Building, the Michigan Building would be in the fashionable Queen Anne style, whose elaborate decoration and eclectic rambling form, complete with turrets and towers, precluded any possibility of plainness. The front facade featured a large, square clock tower. Dormers in the high-pitched shingle roof lighted the third story, designated as the employees' sleeping quarters. From the front entry, a vestibule led into the main rotunda. To the left lay the gentlemen's reading room and reception room; to the right, the ladies' parlor and retiring rooms. A double staircase at the rear led to the second floor's grand hall, assembly room and massive exhibition room.

In April the board published proposals for construction bids in Detroit, Grand Rapids and Saginaw newspapers. On 11 May the managers awarded the building contract to a Grand Rapids firm for $20,392.00. That amount did not include wiring, painting, glass, lathing, plastering or finishing the interior of the structure. As a gang of master carpenters from Grand Rapids hammered Michigan lumber into a majestic Queen Anne structure during the summer of 1892, the board solicited finishing materials. Sensing a good promotional opportunity, Michigan firms responded generously.

The Alabastine Company of Grand Rapids furnished all the necessary plastering material, and

Saginaw contributed furnishings and woodwork for a "Gentleman's Parlor" in the Michigan Building.

Berry Brothers of Detroit applied the varnish and hard oil free. Nels Johnson of Manistee loaned one of his four-faced tower clocks. The Grand Rapids-based Widdicomb Mantel Company installed a large oak mantel in the main rotunda. Detroit's Farrand and Votey Organ Company furnished a $20,000 pipe organ, and Muskegon's Chase Piano Company and Grand Rapids' Bissell Carpet Sweeper Company donated samples of their best lines. The Detroit Safe Company hoisted a large vault into the secretary's office, and Henry A. Newland and Company, also of Detroit, mounted a case of stuffed wolverines.

The City of Grand Rapids finished and furnished the ladies' parlor, which gained a reputation as "the most exquisite room in Jackson Park." Saginaw took on the gentlemen's parlor. William B. Mershon, proprietor of a hardwood factory, lavished $3,000 to render the Saginaw Room a beautiful exhibit of finely tooled woodwork. Muskegon finished the gentlemen's reading room with alabastine plaster and a selection of custom-built, leather-seated library furniture. Over a dozen Grand Rapids furniture makers placed their best wares throughout the building. James B. Angell, president of the University of Michigan, sent his collection of stuffed Michigan game birds; the Belding Silk Works wove a special United States flag; and George W. Kirkbridge, a disabled veteran from Grand Rapids, spent months whittling out parquet maps of the United States and Michigan with each state and county carefully carved out of a different wood. President Weston collected 225 framed portraits of Michigan officials and commissioned a 12 foot x 14 foot watercolor perspective map of the state.

On 29 April 1893 the Michigan Building, "generous in proportions, dignified in construction and graceful in outlines," stood complete. "Rich and ornate in interior finish and furnishings, its large and handsome halls were admirably equipped with everything required for the comfort or convenience of visitors." Only five state buildings exceeded Michigan's in size and but four in cost. The managers festooned the exterior with gay bunting, carefully adjusted the hundreds of framed pictures, laid a "brisk log fire in the huge fireplace of the main rotunda" and awaited the arrival of "three special trains of Wagner sleepers" filled with state officials. When Governor Rich and his staff approached the building, Prince's Lansing Orchestra "furnished delightful strains of music." Following speeches by Weston, Governor Rich, President Angell and Michigan Speaker of the House William A. Tateum, plus a long, terrible poem by S. B. McCracken of Detroit, the board proudly presented its handiwork to the people of the State of Michigan.

The exposition officially opened on 1 May, and Michiganians streamed into the "White City." The Lake Shore Route and other railroads offered special excursion fares. The Graham and Morton Steamship Line conveyed visitors via St. Joseph and Benton Harbor.

Despite the severe industrial depression that began in the summer of 1893, one out of every six people in the country managed to see the fair. The total paid admission for the six-month season reached 27,529,400. A trip to the fair was certainly reasonable by modern standards. Chicago hotels charged $1.00 to $3.00 per night. Admission to the fair cost 50 cents for adults and 25 cents for children. Visitors could "secure a good luncheon" for a quarter and a good dinner for 35 cents to 60 cents. Excluding Illinois, Weston reported that Michigan led all states in attendance with a total of 2,200,000 visitors. However, since the state's population in 1890 stood at 2,093,889, he probably was referring to paid admissions. In addition to the Michigan Building,

Michigan lumbermen displayed the largest load of logs ever pulled by horses at the World's Fair.

which visitors remembered as "a complete, homelike, state club house, with more genuine, broad gauge hospitality and fewer don't cards, bolts or bars than any state headquarters on the grounds," there were plenty of other Michigan-generated attractions to view.

Michigan lumberman intended that the world note their state's national leadership in lumber and sawmill products, hardwood forests, hardwood manufacturers and furniture. They added $10,000 to the $5,000 earmarked for forestry exhibits, providing furnishings and wood work for the Michigan Building and a major exhibit in the Forestry Building. The 528 foot x 208 foot Forestry Building, sided with wood slabs and thatched with bark, stood on the Lake Michigan shore at the extreme southern tip of the fairgrounds. Michigan supplied massive white pine, basswood and maple tree trunks as columns for the veranda of the huge log shanty. Michigan's 50 foot x 60 foot forestry exhibit claimed the hall's most prominent position.

In another section of the exposition, Henry J. Heinz touted his 57 varieties by passing out miniature metallic pickles, but Michigan's magic number was 56. Its exhibit featured three-foot sections of the state's fifty-six varieties of commercial wood, fifty-six glass jars of their seeds and a birchbark bookcase with a fifty-six-volume woodblock library. Charles A. Hibbard and Son of Pequaming displayed a 4 foot x 18 foot plank of solid white pine, the largest at the fair. Another white pine plank, 38 inches x 24 feet, supported an arrangement of manufactured articles including shingles, hoops, barrels, baskets, handles, whiffletrees and croquet sets. Professor Albert J. Cook of the Michigan Agricultural College provided mounted specimens of every known insect injurious to trees. Michigan crowded 3,380 examples of wood and wooden articles into the exhibit. A sign advised visitors, "Woods which will not stand handling will not bear using. Michigan woods are not that kind. Handle them all you wish. This means you."

Michigan won 26 awards for its forestry exhibits, 16 more than any other state. The famed German gunmaker, Friedrich Alfred Krupp, reportedly visited the Michigan exhibit several times in search of timber suitable for gun carriages. Morley Brothers of Saginaw displayed their lumbering tools across the hall from the official exhibit. Farther down the aisle, the Berry Brothers erected one of the most popular forestry exhibits—a gigantic five inch thick 16 foot five inch by 12 foot nine inch plank cut from a California redwood tree and polished on one side with their celebrated Hard Oil Finish.

Three blocks west of the Forestry Building, Michigan lumbermen constructed a popular outdoor attraction, a full-sized replica of a logging camp. Grand Rapids architect George L. Stone designed a 22 foot x 60 foot log cabin roofed with hemlock tiles. The shanty housed a display of every tool used in Michigan logging. Silas Overpack of Manistee sent a set of his big wheels to demonstrate how logs were pulled out of the woods. Nearby, on a length of track, stood a logging locomotive and two loaded logging cars. The pride of the exhibit was a bob sleigh bearing a "champion load" of 18-foot-long white pine logs, which scaled 36,055 feet. The Thomas Nestor estate had hauled this "largest load of logs ever pulled by one span of horses" to the railroad in Baraga County on February 26, 1893.

Michigan farmers were not about to be bested by the lumbermen. They concentrated on a 2,000-square-foot display area located near the center of the 500 foot x 800 foot Palace of Agriculture. They built a 16-foot-square "temple" with finely paneled walls and arched entrances. Thirty-two feet above the floor, a realistic model of Michigan's coat of arms, including

The Michigan Mineral exhibit featured a huge stone arch which was later moved to Grand Rapids' John Ball Park.

stuffed "large, fine Michigan deer with antlers" and an eagle, surmounted the temple dome. Some 260 farmers from 40 counties contributed 5,236 labeled samples of farm products for display within the temple. "Festoons of grain, grasses, and evergreen" hung from the ceiling over pyramids of choice corn ears, glass jars of seeds and grain, sheaves of wheat and oats in the straw, 38 jars of representative Michigan soils, and wax models of fruit and vegetables. On the wall hung photographs of the state's "farm mansions." David Woodman of Paw Paw had plaited corn husks and ears into figures of a man, a woman, a boy and a girl. His "grain family" and the Kalamazoo-based A. M. Todd Company's "promiscuous exhibit" of essential oils attracted special attention. Despite fierce competition from California, which displayed a life-sized statue of a knight on horseback completely made of dried prunes, Michigan's exhibit was one of the most popular in the Agricultural Palace.

Within the 700 foot x 350 foot Mines and Mining Building, the state's mining interests also faced flashy competition. Pennsylvania erected a model of Cleopatra's Needle in anthracite coal; Louisiana sent a statue of Lot's wife carved out of rock salt; and Montana cast in solid silver a seven-foot-tall Justice modeled after popular New York actress Ada Rehan. Michigan Mineral Resources Manager Peter White commissioned Marquette architects Charlton and Gilbert to design a massive stone arch as the focal point of Michigan's 50 foot x 60 foot exhibit area. Stonemasons fashioned the 25-foot-high portal out of reddish sandstone from the Marquette area. Statues of the goddess Victory and two miners crowned the arch.

Visitors passing through the lithic masterpiece saw 1,909 specimens of Michigan minerals and ores, including two record masses of native cooper weighing 8,500 pounds and 6,200 pounds. The

Duluth, South Shore and Atlantic Railroad exhibited a sectional working model of its Number Four ore dock at Marquette. The Cleveland Cliffs Iron Company provided cross-sectional models of soft- and hard-ore mines that were 17 feet long and 10 feet high. The Calumet and Hecla Company obliged with a working model of its shaft and rockhouse, finely designed with each pipe, pulley and screw made to scale. The Michigan Mineral Exhibit received more awards than that of any other state. Michigan's gypsum producers also proudly reported supplying over 40,000 barrels of gypsum and plaster used in making staff, the stucco-like material that covered the exhibition halls.

The 787 foot x 1,687 foot Manufacturers and Liberal Arts Building, the biggest structure at the fair, required the greatest share of Michigan gypsum. Its 202-foot-high roof enclosed over 40 acres of floor space. Steel trusses weighing 12 million pounds, 30,000 panes of glass, 50 tons of paint, 3 million feet of wood flooring, and 5 boxcars of nails went into what was the largest building the world had ever seen. Michigan firms placed displays throughout the structure. Award-winning Michigan exhibitors included Saginaw's Wickes Brothers with their steam boilers, the Alpena Spool Company, Jackson's Coronet Corset Company and Hay & Todd, celebrated for their Ypsilanti long underwear. From Detroit the E. T. Barnum Company displayed fancy iron railings, while Major Hazen Pingree's firm won an award for shoes. The Chase Brothers Piano Company of Muskegon constructed an opulent booth complete with a mirrored ceiling to reflect their prize Michigan birdseye maple piano. Grand Rapids contributed displays from the Goshen Sweeper Company and a dozen furniture companies. Kalamazoo boasted swords and fraternal regalia from Henderson Ames, the Upjohn Company's friable pills and the Asylum for the Insane's blank books. Providing balance to Battle

Creek Sanitarium Superintendent John Harvey Kellogg's award-winning exhibit of fiendish exercise inventions were the remedial appliances from Lansing's Marvin Truss Company.

A variety of the state's educational institutions placed exhibits in the Manufacturers and Liberal Arts Building. In 1891, State Superintendent of Public Instruction Ferris S. Fitch asked the Board of World's Fair Managers for $10,000 for a first-class exhibit. They offered him $1,000. Fitch decided to help finance the school children's exhibit by asking each student to contribute a penny. On Washington's Birthday in 1892 thousands of students across Michigan brought pennies to school and inscribed their names on a "roll of honor." Fitch collected $4,190.44 from the children and bound their signatures in six volumes for display at the fair. Unfortunately, when Lansing's Central Michigan Savings Bank failed in 1892, half the children's pennies were lost. But the state legislature came to the rescue, passing a special appropriation of $2,000. Fitch collected examples of the students' best work and displayed them in the South gallery of the huge hall. Their efforts netted five awards.

Fair officials allocated 2,700 square feet in the Manufacturers and Liberal Arts building to the University of Michigan, a space second in size only to that for Harvard University. Students filled the display with topographical maps of the campus, hundreds of photographs of classes, a bookcase of faculty publications, a miniature machine shop and a mounted group of rare Philippine water buffalo. The Michigan Agricultural College devoted its 25 foot x 50 foot area to models of horse teeth; mounted cow, horse and sheep skeletons; a dissected horse; prime examples from freshmen wood shop; and 54 cases of insects pinned by Lansing students. In addition, an 85-man contingent (two companies and the band of

Michigan military cadets from Orchard Lake escorted Princess Eulalia when she arrived from Spain.

the school's Battalion of Cadets) encamped at the fairgrounds for a week in August.

The Michigan Military Academy of Orchard Lake also sent cadets to the fair. During the first two weeks of June 1893, some 140 of them camped out at the western end of the Midway Plaisance, marched to exhibits "in a systematic way" each morning and held drills and dress parades in the afternoon. On 15 June fair goers watched as cadets—dressed in flashy gray and white uniforms, crimson sashes and plumed headgear—held graduation exercises.

The cadets camped on one of the tamer portions of the Midway, a mile-long strip that connected Jackson Park and Washington Park. This grandmother of all midways was one of the most memorable parts of the exposition. Along its cosmopolitan course lay Hagenbeck's Animal Show, the Ottoman Arab Wild East Show, a half-sized replica of the Blarney Castle and a Cairo street where long lines of people queued up to ogle Little Egypt's gyrations at the Cairo Theatre. Entrepreneurs from around the globe imported exotic nationals to stock Lapland, Turkish, Jahore, South Sea Islander, Javanese, German, Algerian and Chinese villages. A placard at the entrance to the Dahomey village urged visitors not to pique the natives with questions about their former cannibalism.

Before visitors reached the gates of the exposition proper, they wended their way through this confusing international hubbub. Mary S. Stevens, wife of the secretary to the Michigan World's Fair Board, recording the sounds and sights of a trip up the Midway:

"Here's where you get yer fifteen-cent lunch."

"Here's yer sisslin' hot Frankforts; three for ten cents. Last yer all day." (Yes, a lifetime.)

"Here's yer ice cold lemernade, like yer mother useter made. It's makin' while yer waitin.'"

"Smoked glasses make yer handsome; save yer eyes. Folks struck blind, deaf and dumb, ef they be goin' inter the grounds without these beautifiers."

"Here's yer 'ficial catalogue. Can't find the buildin's nor nothin' in 'um if yer don't buy."

An Italian played on an accordion "Ta-ra-ra-a-boom-de-ay," singing a jargon of words sounding like "Hornica-snookery-hornica-snook," to the end of the air, while a child danced among the people, kicking their shins and holding out her tambourine for pennies.

"Ladies and gentlemen, don't go by the greatest show on earth. Ye'll regret it to yer dyin' day. Here's where ye'll see the two-headed pig, the double twisted Lord-a-massa, the Indian-rubber man, who stretches his chist skin over his hull face; had the stretchinest skin in the worl'."

At the center of the Midway, America's anwer to the Eiffel Tower, the original Ferris Wheel, rose to a height of 264 feet. George W. Ferris had designed his engineering marvel to resemble a gigantic bicycle wheel—825 feet in circumference. The 1,220-ton wheel supported 36 gondolas the size of boxcars, and each held 40 passengers. Two 1,000-horsepower steam engines turned the wheel two revolutions every 20 minutes. As Mary Stevens paid her 50 cents for a ticket she overheard an old lady, who refused to accompany her group, protest, "I have a through ticket for Heaven, and I do not mean to go halfway there and return."

Another Midway attraction was Chief Sitting

Board of World's Fair Managers for Michigan, 1895.

E.H. BELDEN, Vice President. — J.W. FLYNN, Treasurer. — PETER WHITE, Manager. — GOVERNOR E.B. WINANS, Ex-Officio Manager. — J.M. WESTON, President. — GOVERNOR JOHN T. RICH, Ex-Officio Manager. — MRS. J.A. POND, Manager. — MARK W. STEVENS, Secretary. — MRS. J.S. VALENTINE, Manager.

Michigan's World's Fair managers accomplished their task with distinction.

Bull's log cabin—the very cabin where he had been killed. In his place presided Rain-in-the-Face, who, according to Mary Stevens, "cut out the heart and drank the blood of the noble Tom Custer, at the same time killing daring, dashing, brave General Custer, with the help of his band of howling savages, who sacrificed Calhoun, and a large number of grave companions, many of whom belonged to Michigan." As Stevens stared at the crippled Indian, she heard another spectator tell him, "I'm glad you're maimed for life, and will never walk again without a crutch, and that you're situated so that the opportunity will never again be presented to take the lives of such as the Custers, and his brave army."

To the west of Sitting Bull's log cabin, just down the road from the California Ostrich Farm and the Captive Balloon Park, lay the American Indian Village. There visitors could purchase one of Simon Pokagon's miniature birchbark pamphlets for 50 cents. Chief Pokagon of Hartford, Michigan, had penned "The Red Man's Greeting," lamenting America's failure to properly honor Indians at the exposition. Pokagon, son of Leopold Pokagon, the Potawatomi chief who signed the 1833 Chicago treaty that deeded to the white man millions of acres of ancestral land including the site which became the fairgrounds, was invited as a guest of honor during the exposition's Chicago Week. On 9 October, Chicago Day, as 750,000 visitors thronged the fairgrounds, Pokagon addressed the crowd and rang the "new liberty bell" for the first time. In the afternoon he umpired a lacrosse game between Canadian Iroquois and Potawatomi held in the stock pavilion. That evening he rode atop a float depicting a heroic scene from the 1812 Indian massacre at Fort Dearborn.

Throughout the fair's six months, other states and countries were honored. Michigan Days were 13-14

245

September.   Responding to Governor Rich's proclamation urging Michigan citizens to visit the fair on those days, railroad and steamship lines offered reduced rates. Over 35,000 Michiganians arrived for the festivities. The grand day began at 9:00 A. M. with a concert on the green by the West Point Military Academy Cadet Band. At 10:00 A. M. The oratorical exercises commenced on a platform erected at the north end of the gaily decorated Michigan Building. The principal speaker, Thomas W. Palmer, former U. S. senator from Detroit and president of the exposition, began his address:

> It is a good thing to be born. It is a good thing to look upon the sun, to be one among neighbors, to be a citizen of a community, of a town or a city, of a state, of a nation; but it is better than all to be a man, and if one is a man he is certain to recognize the obligations which all the above conditions imply.

Several thousand words later, Palmer reached the crescendo of his rhetorical fervor:

> The state of Cass, Houghton, Tappan, Chandler, Watson, Howard and Custer, dead, and many equally broad, bright and courageous living, may well stand in line of the final dress parade of the nineteenth century and challenge inspection. If a peninsula is sought fertile in honor, morals, loyalty, material resources, education and all forces that make for human betterment, let them look around our State.

Then, as one observer noted, "the band played, the crowd cheered and everybody seemed patriotic and happy."

Following Palmer's speech, the crowd heard short

talks by former Governors Josiah Begole and Russell Alger, by Frederick Douglass, who had resided in Detroit during the 1850s, and by 85-year-old Laura Haviland, the underground railroad agent from Adrian. At 2:00 P. M. the Chase Brothers Piano Company put on a concert, while a group of Ann Arbor students added some college songs and a "few terrific college yells." That evening everyone repaired to the lakefront to savor an exhibition of fireworks arranged by exposition authorities to honor Michigan.

A few short weeks later, the world's fair was over. The recent assassination of Chicago Mayor Carter Harrison lent a somber mood to the closing ceremonies on 30 October. Mary Stevens echoed the nation's assessment of the exposition. "There never was and may never again be anything so grand of like interest that will be as uplifting and ennobling."

Amid considerable discussion of preserving the Columbian Exposition as a permanent exhibit and replacing the temporary staff exteriors of the exhibition walls with more durable material, fire destroyed the majority of the huge structures. The managers put the glorious Michigan Building up for wrecking bids. The Chicago House Wrecking Company wanted $1,493 to remove the building, but the Davis and Johnson Company took a better look at the fancy woodwork and offered to pay the board $1,500, the best price for any building of its size.

Many of Michigan's exhibits found new homes among the state's institutions. The state library accessioned the school children's six-volume roll of honor. The 225 half-toned engravings of state officials from the Michigan Building wound up at the state capitol. The Michigan Agricultural College shipped the entire agricultural exhibit back to its museum. The model of the Calumet and Hecla Mine went to the University of Michigan; the Marquette ore dock model, to the Michigan School of Mines (now Michigan Technological University) at Houghton; and the massive sandstone arch, to John Ball Park in Grand Rapids. Wealthy Philadelphia newspaperman George W. Childs bought the logging cabin as the best example of rustic architecture at the fair.

The general consensus of those who saw the fair was that those who had missed it were an unfortunate lot. Mary W. Brender returned to Otsego to pen an epic, *Our First Columbian,* for the "children who were unable to attend the World's Fair." Mary Stevens published a 31-page pamphlet, *A Lecture on What You Missed in Not Visiting the World's Fair* and a 382-page volume, *Six Months at the World's Fair.* Stevens sadly wrote, "The glory and grandeur of the beautiful 'White City,' fraught with happy recollections, is forever a thing of the past." But Michigan could be rightfully proud of its role in creating "the fairest city that ever the sun shown on."

"Get Out and Get Under": Automotive Pioneers in Kalamazoo

Ransom Olds ran a "Merry Oldsmobile" up the steps of the capitol in Lansing, ca. 1903.

The strange little contraption clanked and clattered along the cedar-block paving of downtown Kalamazoo. Big eyed, George W. Taylor clutched the tiller with white-knuckled hands as he steered the steam-powered Locomobile toward his Michigan Avenue haberdashery. Hissing like an angry goose, Kalamazoo's first horseless carriage left a wake of rearing steeds, cursing teamsters, and startled pedestrians.

Taylor's shiny new 1899 Locomobile had arrived from the plant in Newton, Massachusetts, on January 24, 1900. Plenty of Kalamazooans thought the "Loco" in the name perfectly appropriate. It was plain crazy to disturb the peace and quiet of the city with that infernal machine. Besides, it could not compete with real horsepower. Horses would never be replaced.

The "Celery City's" encounter with its first automobile would mirror occurrences in Battle Creek, Jackson, Saginaw, Grand Rapids and other booming turn-of-the-century Michigan communities. Over the course of the succeeding decade, they, like Kalamazoo, would also learn to accept the gasoline powered phenomena which would revolutionize American society as well as Michigan's economy.

Five months after he introduced Kalamazoo to gasoline exhaust fumes, clothier Taylor had had enough of runaway teams and jeering crowds. He sold his Locomobile to Dr. William E. Upjohn, who intended to use it to deliver friable pills and other popular remedies manufactured by his thriving Upjohn Pill and Granule Company.

Upjohn and Taylor, Kalamazoo's pioneer motorists, were members of a very small fraternity in 1900. At year's end there were only 8,000 automobiles in the entire country compared to 17 million horses. The only real threat to equine dominance seemed to be the bicycle craze that had swept the nation during the

"Gay Nineties."

In 1892 two young bicycle mechanics, J. Frank and Charles Duryea, fashioned the first American-built car. Their improved "Buggyaut" won the original American motor race held on Thanksgiving 1895 in Chicago. The following winter, the Duryea Motor Wagon Company constructed 13 vehicles, the first automobiles regularly manufactured for sale in the U. S.

In spite of primitive roads that were unfit for vehicular travel, America was catching automotive fever. Across the land, monkey-wrench mechanics tinkered with ungainly contraptions calculated to launch an industry. Many were hardly more than buggies with a little engine strapped on.

In 1896 Charles B. King and, a few months later, Henry Ford, built and ran horseless carriages on the streets of Detroit. By 1900 bold entrepreneurs had launched scores of automobile factories. Michigan claimed two, both in Detroit. Ransom E. Olds was busy building his popular "Merry Oldsmobiles." His smaller rival, the Detroit Automobile Company, went bankrupt before the year's end, despite the efforts of it chief engineer, Henry Ford.

Like the Duryea brothers, many of the first automobile makers had cut their mechanical teeth on bicycles. Alexander Winton left his Cleveland bicycle shop to build motorcycles, the Winton car, and to win recognition as one of America's best race drivers. Col. Albert A. Pope, who had made millions of dollars on his famous Columbia bicycles, started a number of automobile companies. Two other bicycle-building brothers, Orville and Wilbur Wright, turned their attention to more lofty endeavors.

Kalamazoo's pioneer automakers, Maurice and Clarence Blood, also sprang from the bicycle tradition. The Blood brothers had established the Kalamazoo Cycle Company on North Rose Street in 1891 to

251

Maurice and Charles Blood posed in one of their Kalamazoo made automobiles in front of Bronson Park, ca. 1903

manufacture "Fortune" brand bicycles and a unique bicycle basket they had invented. The Fortune bicycle proved popular, but the basket was a flop—too far ahead of its time.

Kalamazoo's dominant vehicle manufacturers during the 1890s, however, were buggy and carriage factories. in 1895, no less than 11 companies employed more than 800 skilled workers. Kalamazoo was one of the midwest's leading producers of horse-drawn vehicles.

The Blood brothers thought Kalamazoo might well parlay its aptitude for carriage making into automobile manufacturing. Maurice Blood made quite a splash in the October 20, 1900, edition of the *Kalamazoo Telegraph* when he predicted that the automobile industry would become one of the country's largest, and Kalamazoo might become as big an automobile center as it had for buggies. Windmills, sleds, corsets, and celery seemed a better bet to most Kalamazooans, but the Blood brothers were determined to make Maurice's prophecy come true.

The Bloods' Kalamazoo Cycle Company expanded its services to become the area's first automobile dealership. In April, 1901, it sold a new Mobile steam car made in New York to Oscar K. Buckhout, a prosperous local manufacturer of embalming fluids. With its buggy-type top up, Buckhout's ungainly looking Mobile was actually higher than it was long. Nevertheless it whistled along at 25 miles per hour. Other early automotive converts included Alderman H. E. Congdon, who recommended that the city purchase an electric-powered ambulance to eliminate the expense of horses.

By the spring of 1902, the Blood brothers had their own handmade automobile on the road. That prototype showed its bicycle heritage and looked more appropriate for the golf course than the highway. Powered by a one-cylinder, air-cooled engine, it seated two passengers, weighed 360 pounds, and had a wheel base of 48 inches. The Blood brothers drove the little novelty more than 3,000 dusty miles that summer.

"So you are going to get an automobile?" "Yes," answered the man who is always thinking of his health. "My doctor says I must walk more." So ran a contemporary bon mot, and the automobile entered the stream of American consciousness as a facetious and undependable diversion, a rich man's toy, and a sport to be undertaken by only the hardy. Early motoring ranked as one of the more strenuous athletic endeavors. Cantankerous engines and thin-skinned pneumatic tires coupled with horrible roads decreed that every motorist be a mechanic. Goggles, leather, gloves, and linen dusters were more necessity than style. "Get a horse" and "Get out and get under" became common roadside slogans.

Now-mundane automotive events qualified as news in 1902. On May 18 the *KalamazooTelegraph* reported that an auto party of eight in one vehicle had passed through the city during a hard rain en route to Otsego. Windshield wipers, even the manually operated kind, were yet to be invented. The stalwart motorists had left South Bend at 7:30 a.m. and reached Kalamazoo eight and a half hours later.

Rough driving conditions did little to stem the automotive tide in Kalamazoo. The *Telegraph* noted on May 27, 1902, that penny-arcade-machine manufacturer Arthur L. Pratt's new Packard had arrived from Warren, Ohio, and it was a "hummer."

On August 1 of that year, Dr. Edward Ames became Kalamazoo's first automotive physician when he began using his gasoline-powered Locomobile to make house calls. Doctors, more than any other profession, eagerly adapted automobiles to their practices. By 1905, eight local healers had swapped

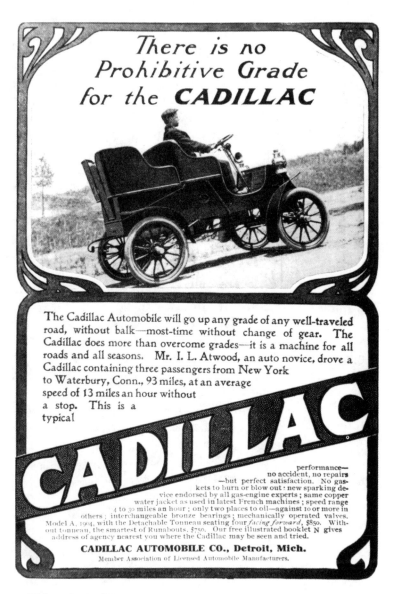

There is no
Prohibitive Grade
for the **CADILLAC**

The Cadillac Automobile will go up any grade of any well-traveled road, without balk—most-time without change of gear. The Cadillac does more than overcome grades—it is a machine for all roads and all seasons. Mr. I. L. Atwood, an auto novice, drove a Cadillac containing three passengers from New York to Waterbury, Conn., 93 miles, at an average speed of 13 miles an hour without a stop. This is a typical

CADILLAC

performance—
no accident, no repairs
—but perfect satisfaction. No gaskets to burn or blow out : new sparking device endorsed by all gas-engine experts ; same copper water jacket as used in latest French machines ; speed range 4 to 30 miles an hour ; only two places to oil—against 10 or more in others ; interchangeable bronze bearings ; mechanically operated valves. Model A, 1904, with the Detachable Tonneau seating four *facing forward*, $850. Without tonneau, the smartest of Runabouts, $750. Our free illustrated booklet N gives address of agency nearest you where the Cadillac may be seen and tried.

CADILLAC AUTOMOBILE CO., Detroit, Mich.
Member Association of Licensed Automobile Manufacturers.

This 1904 Cadillac ad promised it would "go up any grade of well traveled road without balk."

255

one-horse buggies for horseless carriages. Although one, "Dr." Dirk P. Yonkerman was actually a veterinarian masquerading as a physician to better market his patent-medicine frauds, but that's another story.

Automobiles also began to create a greater need for physicians. Five Kalamazoo youths, who had gone to Battle Creek for a 1902 Labor Day celebration, became the first local accident victims when Battle Creek Alderman C. M. McConnell lost control of his car and plowed into the crowd. In 1904 George W. Parker set the unfortunate precedent of becoming Kalamazoo's first automotive fatality.

Equine trepidation lay at the root of many early automotive mishaps. On October 21, 1902, Arthur Pratt's red Packard made news again when the "hummer" frightened a horse which then overturned its buggy. Over in Battle Creek, Seventh Day Adventist Elder Uriah Smith thought he had the solution when he mounted a wooden horse's head on the hood of his auto. It did not work.

Contemporary opinion usually sided with horseflesh against the noisy and smoky motor cars. Compared to the down-to-earth pollution left by the horse, gasoline fumes assailed the nostrils of horse and man alike.

The 1905 volume, *Chauffeur Chaff,* probably the first automobile joke book, contained plenty of humorous anecdotes such as:

"That'll be a powerful machine," said a native of the north of Scotland to a motorist.
"Yes, it's a splendid car," proudly replied the owner.
"I suppose a car like that will be nearly a hundred horsepower?" suggested the countryman.
"Oh no," said the motorist modestly. "It is only ten horse! A hundred horsepower car would be

much larger."

"I wasn't going by size," the Highlander explained dryly. "I was going by the smell of it."

Despite its unfortunate accident record, the year 1902 proved propitious for the local automobile industry. Two Kalamazoo firms joined the ranks of the dozen or so Michigan-based automobile manufacturers. On January 4, 1902, M. B. Williams and W. B. Cannon formed the Automatic Machine Company to make automobile gas engines, clutches, and launches. Williams supplied the factory space in the old Williams Manufacturing Company plant at Edwards and Water streets, and Cannon the inventive skills. Cannon was still working on the prototype when his company merged with the Burtt Manufacturing Company in October of 1902. The following year Burtt went into production of what Cannon called "The Kalamazoo" automobile.

By 1904 the company marketed an improved model variously called the "Celebrated Cannon" and the "Cannon Flyer." They were available in three styles ranging in price from $650 to $1,350. Burtt's advertising copy rationalized "the fact that this concern is way behind in filling orders is a clear indication of the great demand for these machines." The following year 17 employees produced $20,900 worth of automobiles.

The state factory inspector reported Burtt was developing a new automobile with a full, ball-bearing crankshaft and 40-horsepower engine. The company had grown out of its quarters and was contemplating a large new factory. But something went askew with the grandiose plans. In 1906 Burtt reduced its work force to nine and within two years no longer manufactured automobiles.

Meanwhile the Blood brothers continued their automotive experimentation. In October 1902 they announced another improved light automobile that would sell for $400. On December 30, 1902, Frank and Charles Fuller joined the firm, which then reorganized as the Michigan Automotive Company. The Fuller brothers, although fresh from a Battle Creek cereal-boom debacle with their ill-fated Korn Krisp company, whose product rapidly grew rancid on store shelves because it contained too much oil, brought important organizational and advertising savvy to the partnership.

The Michigan Automobile Company began marketing automobiles in 1903. The improved Michigan two-seater, as designed by the Blood brothers, weighed only 425 pounds and reputedly got 100 miles to the gallon of fuel. At $450, it was one of the cheapest cars in America at the time. Later the company introduced a larger four-seater model powered by a two-cylinder engine that sold for $1,250.

Although the Blood brothers withdrew from the Michigan Automobile Company after a year, prospects seemed bright for the Fullers. In November 1904, they announced a new side-entrance car called the Model E Michigan and reported that business was so good the plant was running overtime.

By the following year, the Michigan Automobile Company had added W. E. Upjohn, the local automobile pioneer, to its roster of officers as treasurer. At the new brick plant located on the northeast corner of Prouty and North Pitcher streets, 56 workers turned out $65,000 worth of Michigans in 1905. One half of the output, the Fullers proudly announced in 1906, had been sold in the Kalamazoo area.

But as more and more entrepreneurs entered the highly competitive automobile industry, business began to lag for the Michigan Automobile Company. In 1907 only 44 employees drew pay envelopes, and the following year another dozen were laid off. The

By 1904 Oldsmobile ads boasted that over 20,000 of the vehicles were in actual service.

last year for the Michigan company was 1908. But the Fullers remained in business by specializing in a component they made particularly well— transmissions.

During the first decade of the 20th century, as the hectic scramble for success in the automobile industry blossomed into motor mania, hundreds of makes of cars beguiled consumers. Eventually American would produce more than 2,500 brands of automobiles. Some came and went so fast their history was lost in the shuffle. A few tantalizing bits of evidence remain, for example, concerning another "Kalamazoo" car that made a brief appearance in 1903.

M. Henry Lane and Frank. B. Lay, proprietors of the city's largest horse-drawn-vehicle factory, the Michigan Buggy Company, evidently decided to hedge their bet and by adding automobiles to the company's popular line of buggies, "Tony Pony" vehicles, and cutters.

In February 1903 Lane and Lay began promoting a concept "to make automobiles on a large scale." They planned a 640-pound car that would go 15 miles per hour. On July 16, the *Telegraph* announced that the firm would name its automobile the "Kalamazoo." The first cars, available in runabout and touring styles, would be out within the week. If they ever actually became available, all traces have disappeared. The fate of that "Kalamazoo" remains a mystery.

Regardless of Lane and Lay's automotive fiasco, interest in automobiles continued strong in Kalamazoo. On May 29, 1903, Locher and Robb, operators of the new Cadillac agency, made their first sale to Dr. Francis J. Welsh. That same month Frederick N. Rowley, cashier of the First National Bank, ordered a 24-horsepower automobile of an unknown make. That June Archibald Campbell proudly honked his way through the city in his new Orient Buckboard car. The Rev. E. J. Blekkink, progressive pastor of the Second Reformed Church, shocked his congregation in July with a five-horse-power auto he intended to "use for church work."

Kalamazoo marveled at the daring of E. C. Adams and F. H. Wilson when they drove from Battle Creek to Kalamazoo in a little more than two hours on March 17, 1904. Hundreds of Kalamazooans lined the streets for Kalamazoo's first automobile parade that featured 15 cars on July 2. But the major automotive milestone of 1904 was the unveiling of the Blood brothers' new car.

After leaving the Michigan Automobile Company and the Fullers in early 1904, Maurice and Clarence Blood established the Blood Brothers Automobile and Machine Company on North Edwards Street. In June they had the prototype of their new "side entrance tonneau touring car" on the road. It was radically different from their diminutive early models. Powered by a 16-horse-power engine, the new Blood had a wheel base of 90 inches and weighed 1,700 pounds. Identical front and rear seats could carry six passengers. A unique design enabled easy removal of the rear seat for conversion into a type of pickup truck. The car sold for $1,500.

The Cycle and Automotive Trade Journal of November 1904, carried a glowing review of the Blood based on a successful road test. The Blood brothers manufactured and sold several of their new models during 1904 and 1905. But by 1906 the Bloods also had fallen victim to the fiercely competitive automobile market. Like the Fuller's, the renamed Blood Brothers Machine Company continued production of its superior specialty—universal joints—ultimately in Allegan.

"Motoring has been overdone and people are tiring of it in droves. The second-hand auto has become a real article of commerce," the *Telegraph* quoted a local dealer on January 5, 1905. But then,

261

contemporary car dealers also get glum in January.

Actually, 1905 marked a dramatic surge in Kalamazoo's transition to the automobile age. Even horse-livery operators, who seemingly had the most to lose, began jumping on the automotive bandwagon. In April Joel Waterbury bought a Michigan for $1,250 and began using it at his East Water Street livery. That same month William Harlow inaugurated another automobile livery. Cars could be rented by the hour or day, and Harlow even furnished drivers.

April 22, 1905, saw the advent of the city's first motor-bus route. Nazareth Academy bought an Oldsmobile bus and operated it between downtown and the academy. "Motorman" M. J. Larkins collected 25 cents for what was then a half-hour trip up steep Gull Road hill.

Later that year Frank Wilson opened Kalamazoo's first automobile garage at 425 E. Michigan Avenue. His entire stock of tools consisted of a bench vise and a box of wrenches. Barrels of gasoline stood in front of the garage. Wilson's son, John, Kalamazoo's first gasoline attendant, measured gas into containers and sloshed it into gas tanks using a funnel. Gasoline sold for nine cents a gallon that year. The initial motor vehicle state law required each garage to post the types of automobiles it expected to repair. Wilson listed Michigan's Oldsmobile, Buick, and Cadillac; Kalamazoo's own Cannon and Michigan; the Rambler made in Kenosha, Wisconsin; and the Elmore from Clyde, Ohio.

James C. Hatfield, treasurer of the Kalamazoo Corset Company, the world's largest producer of those instruments of torture contemporary fashion decreed essential even for lady motorists, formed the Kalamazoo Auto Club in 1905. The organization sought to have a hand in the formation of automobile ordinances in the city.

Accordingly, on June 15, 1905, Michigan's first

Cornelian Light Car

$410
Top and
Windshield
$25 Extra

$410
Top and
Windshield
$25 Extra

The Easiest Rider of Them All

Not a large car whittled down, but a **designed light car.** The following high-grade mechanical features are **built** into this little car:

Full floating rear axle.

Independent spring seat suspension. (Patented and a great feature.)

Stream line body with beautiful and durable baked enamel finish.

Fifteen large set New Departure ball bearings.

Standard tread. 100" wheelbase.

Thirty-one Chrome Vanadium steel special drop forgings

The most simple and the safest steering gear ever devised.

Sliding gear transmission with only three gears and no countershaft. (A real mechanical wonder.)

Sterling overhead valve motor. $2\frac{3}{4}$" x 4"; eighteen horsepower! a thousand pounds!

MECHANICALLY PERFECT

A speedy, easy riding light car, with the punch

BLOOD BROS. MACHINE COMPANY
ALLEGAN, MICHIGAN
Formerly of Kalamazoo

The Blood Brothers built the Cornelian car in Kalamazoo and in Allegan where they relocated in 1914.

automobile laws went into effect. Vehicle licenses cost $2 and the owner had to furnish his own plates, originally made of leather. No operator's license was required. State speed limits were set at eight mph for business districts and 15 mph for residential areas, but motorists could zoom up to 25 mph out in the country. As part of the new regulations, a car census documented 52 cars in Kalamazoo, including eight Michigans, seven Cannons and two Bloods.

Drs. Augustus W. Crane and Caspar K. LaHuis, a couple of "scorchers" as contemporary slang labeled speeders, earned Kalamazoo's first traffic tickets. They were arrested and fined $20 each.

They might well have saved their "scorching" for the city's first automobile race, held at Recreation Park on July 14, 1905. Because so many local physicians owned cars, a doctors' race was held. During the later feature race, the "White Ghost" beat the "Red Devil" and startled spectators with the unprecedented speed of nearly a mile a minute.

A unique event at Kalamazoo's first automobile meet was a "slow race" around the track. The Burtt Manufacturing Company had produced a special Cannon that was one of the largest passenger cars ever built. It weighed 4,500 pounds and a man standing at the rear could not reach the top of the tonneau. Dewitt C. Olin drove the huge Cannon in the slow race.

John Wilson recalled the race in 1925:

The Cannon had a big flywheel which two men could not lift and with a faint chug of the motor the flywheel would turn over and carry the car along at a speed so slow that it almost stood still. When the other cars crossed the line, Olin was not yet in sight down the stretch.

Olin won the event at a speed of less than two

miles per hour. Perhaps the Cannon Flyer would have been more successful if "slow races" had caught on in popularity.

"Why are you so sure your wife will want an automobile for Christmas?"
"Why, there isn't anything that costs more, is there?"

Chauffeur Chaff quipped thusly in 1905. Women might not be able to vote yet but they were beginning to get behind the wheel. Kalamazoo's pioneer woman driver, the wife of "Dr." Dirk P. Yonkerman, the patent medicine huckster, started driving her husband's Cadillac in 1903. Mrs. Winifred Upjohn Smith became the next "automobilette." By August of 1906, a *Kalamazoo Gazette* feature identified five female drivers in the city, including Mrs. Donald Boudeman, Mrs. C. H. Swindell, and Mrs. J. W. Ryder.

As the century wore on, wisecracks about women drivers became the humorous mainstay of male motorists, but in the early days quite a few men needed a little extra driving assistance. The problem of backing a car out of the garage, for example, was ingeniously dealt with by two Kalamazoo motorists. Ira Ransom, president of the American Playing Card Company, installed a turn-table in his South Park Street garage so he would not have to back up his "Merry Oldsmobile." James L. Sebring had a better idea. He built doors on both ends of his garage and drove in from South Street and out onto Park Street.

In 1908 Henry Ford introduced an automobile that would revolutionize the industry—the tough, inexpensive, no-nonsense Model T. "A Ford will go anywhere except in society" became one of many Model T jokes. While Detroit's Ford had launched an empire, Kalamazoo's unrelated namesake did not do so well. The year 1905 found Charles B. Ford operating the Ford Manufacturing Company at the corner of Stockbridge and Fulford avenues. Ford advertised that he made automobiles, pianos, surrey bodies, fanning mills, and wood novelties. The next year, however, saw his line reduced to kitchen cabinets and wood novelties.

For every entrepreneur like the Detroit Ford who made a success in the early automobile industry, scores like the Kalamazoo Ford failed.

Kalamazoo's John Soules offers another example. The 1907 *Kalamazoo City Directory* listed Soules as an inventor who lived with his wife, Millie, on DeWitt Street. Soules made news on June 27, 1907, when the *Telegraph* announced he was "attracting crowds on North Burdick Street" with his auto parcel delivery. The car was being manufactured by the Michigan Automobile Works for the Soules Motor Car Company. The Soules Motor Car Company, however, never showed up in the city directory, and by 1909 John and Millie Soules had disappeared from the city as well.

Kalamazoo held its first automobile show at the National Guard Armory in April 1910. Fourteen exhibitors, ranging from the Indiana made Auburn to the Ohio made White, proudly displayed their prize vehicles. Sadly, not a single locally made car was then in production.

But following a decade of automobile pioneering that had seen several valiant attempts, Kalamazoo automobile manufacturers would pause to catch their breath. But beginning in 1913 and throughout the Roaring 20s, a new set of entrepreneurs would hitch their dreams to a gasoline powered chariot. Michigans, Barleys, Roamers, Checkers, Handley-Knights, Wolverines, and other Kalamazoo-made cars would give Detroit, Flint, and Lansing a pretty good run for their money.

Dr. Crippen, the Killer from Coldwater

Dr. Hawley Harvey Crippen, who hacked his wife's body to pieces.

Capt. Henry Kendall lit his briar pipe, took a couple of satisfying puffs, then glanced out his cabin's porthole. The sight he witnessed nearly caused him to drop his pipe. There behind a lifeboat stood two men holding hands in a most romantic manner! In fact, the younger of the pair "squeezed the other's hand immodestly."

It was July 20, 1910, a considerably less tolerant age, and Kendall, master of the Canadian Pacific emigrant steamer *Montrose* bound from Antwerp to Quebec, was appalled to think of that funny stuff going on aboard his vessel. As he continued to observe the spectacle, the captain, who prided himself on the detective skills he had honed while ferreting out con men on numerous voyages, noticed something even more peculiar about the younger man. His snug fitting suit jacket and trousers were so tight they had split up the back. They were held together with safety pins, and appeared to bulge in the wrong places—for a man, that is. Clearly his duty lay, Kendall concluded, in getting to the bottom of this mystery.

Several hours later, the captain introduced himself to the pair and invited them to join him for lunch. The older of the two, a slight, balding, smooth-shaven man approximately 50 years old, identified himself as John Harvey Robinson. He was, he explained, taking his son to Canada for health reasons. The boy dutifully coughed several times, but when questioned he answered tersely in a high-pitched voice. As Kendall scrutinized the elder Robinson's watery eyes, he noticed the tell-tale red marks on either side of the bridge of his nose indicative of someone who had long worn glasses.

Despite the growing evidence that his mysterious passengers had adopted a disguise, Kendall had the uneasy feeling that he had seen them before.

The newspapers had recently been filled with

sensational stories about a "North London Cellar Murder" and Scotland Yard's frenzied search for the suspects, Dr. Hawley Harvey Crippen and Miss Ethel LeNeve. Like many another armchair detective, Kendall had followed those stories with interest. Could this queer acting duo be the runaway murderers, he pondered?

Midway through the lunch, Kendall excused himself, hastened to their cabin, and rummaged through their meager luggage looking for a clue. He discovered little, other than that the boy's hat was padded with tissue to make it fit and that he had been using a piece ripped from a lady's undergarment for a washcloth—not exactly damning evidence. Still, a possible link between these two and the fugitive murderers bothered Kendall.

Returning to his cabin, he flipped through a pile of newspapers he had saved to read on the voyage until he found a copy of the *Daily Mail* containing the likenesses of the murder suspects. Cutting out a cardboard template in order to mask her luxuriant hairdo, Kendall placed it over the portrait of Ethel LeNeve. Then he carefully chalked out the eyeglasses and moustache from Crippen's photograph. Staring up at him from the newspaper were the exact likenesses of John Harvey Robinson and his son.

The lurid headlines about the cellar murder splashed across newspapers on both sides of the Atlantic during the summer of 1910. They had shocked no group of readers more than the 5,945 residents of Coldwater, the Branch County seat and a community that prided itself on economic success earned via the manufacture of Indian clubs, children's sleds, shoes, cigars, and Kitchell's Liniment, "good for man and beast."

Coldwater boasted a handsome stone public library, low taxes, more than 40 miles of cement sidewalks, and broad, tree-shaded avenues lined with

Main Street in Early Morning, Coldwater, Mich.

Coldwater's Main Street looking west, ca. 1910.

mansions. In short, it was the epitome of a midwestern county seat—a good place to live and raise a family. Unfortunately for the community's good name, however, among those who had grown to manhood there was one, Hawley Harvey Crippen, wanted by Scotland Yard for what it termed "the murder of the century."

The Crippen family name looms large in the annals of Coldwater. Bradley Crippen, patriarch of the clan, had emigrated by covered wagon from western New York to Coldwater in 1835. With him came several family members, including his sons Lorenzo and Philo, Hawley's grandfather. The Crippens all moved into one of the first houses to be constructed in Coldwater, located at the present site of the public library.

Philo and Lorenzo went into partnership and opened a dry goods store and flour mill. Both married and raised families. Philo sired Myron Augustus Crippen, Hawley's father. Later, when Lorenzo and Philo's wife died prematurely, Philo remarried his brother's widow. The family prospered, growing moderately wealthy on real estate ventures, and the Crippens took an active role in the local Methodist church.

Myron succeeded his father as proprietor of the dry goods store, married a local girl, Andresse Skinner, and moved into one of the most imposing Italianate residences in the city located at the corner of Grand and Monroe Streets. In 1862, the couple brought Harley into the world.

Pampered and spoiled by parents and grandparents, Crippen grew into an egotistical and headstrong young man whose ambition was to follow in the steps of his Uncle Bradley, a local family physician. He attended the University of Michigan for a spell, then took his medical degree at the Homeopathic Hospital College in Cleveland, Ohio. After serving his internship at the Hahnemann

271

Hospital in Manhattan, Crippen established a practice as an eye and ear specialist.

At Hahnemann, the 25-year-old Crippen had fallen in love with a student nurse, an Irish lass named Charlotte Jane Bell. Their unhappy marriage ended five years later when Charlotte died of apoplexy. Crippen left the son she had borne him with his parents, who had moved from Coldwater to California, and returned to New York.

Six months later, he met a fashionably plump 19-year-old woman of Polish ancestry who, despite her mediocre talent, believed she was destined to become a great opera star. Swept off his feet by her charms, Crippen married the singer who had taken the stage name of Belle Elmore less than two months after he met her.

Their marital bliss lasted but briefly. Homeopathic medicine, the theory that minute doses of drugs which produce on a healthy person effects similar to the symptoms suffered by the patient could produce a cure, had fallen from favor with the public. Crippen's practice suffered, and soon there was no money for the expensive voice lesson that Belle so badly needed.

The Crippens moved into progressively less respectable apartments, until finally Belle took the bull by the horns. She convinced Crippen that their only chance to rise up in the world lay in his leaving the regular practice of medicine and joining the fraternity of quacks who were earning a good living by gulling the sick with elixirs whose operative components were alcohol, narcotics or both.

Crippen secured a position with Professor Munyon, proprietor of an international quack empire built around Munyon's Pile Cure and other fraudulent concoctions. The doctor from Coldwater proved an able quack and over the succeeding decade he advanced steadily within the Munyon organization.

In 1897, Munyon asked Crippen to take charge of a new London branch of the firm at an annual salary of $10,000, equivalent to more than 20 times that sum in contemporary terms.

Despite their financial windfall, in England the Crippen's marriage enjoyed about as much success as did Belle's musical career. After a debut in a mini-operetta which flopped, Belle entered vaudeville, specializing in singing popular ballads in a high-pitched voice. She also met new friends in the vaudeville circuit, including an ex-prize fighter turned musician from Chicago with whom she struck up a liaison.

When Professor Munyon found out that Crippen was managing his wife's vaudeville career on the side, thereby linking his medicine's reputation with that of a side show, he fired Crippen. Not about to waste the valuable secrets of fleecing the ill he had learned from Munyon, Crippen established a succession of his own patent medicine schemes, including a nerve tonic he called Amorette. Eventually he joined the Drouet Institute for the Deaf, the London branch of a French mail order racket through which sufferers paid through the nose for diagnosis and treatment without ever seeing the doctor in person.

It was at the Drouet Institute in 1903 that Crippen finally met the love of his life in the form of a 17-year-old stenographer named Ethel Clara LeNeve. She also believed that she had found her soul mate, even after she discovered he was married. Over the course of the succeeding seven years, Crippen and Ethel pursued a sedate love affair. Quite naturally, his relationship with Belle suffered an even further decline—the marriage grew more and more intolerable—and then following a late dinner party on January 31, 1910, Belle was seen no more.

Crippen told Belle's coterie of theatrical friends that she had been suddenly called back to America to take care of a sick relative. That explanation might have sufficed had not the love-blinded Crippen begun to make a series of foolish mistakes. For one thing, six weeks after Belle's disappearance, Ethel moved in with Crippen.

Suspicions were further aroused when one night a next-door neighbor saw in front of a lighted upstairs window Ethel trying on Belle's costumes. Worse yet, Ethel appeared in public wearing Belle's favorite jeweled brooch. Crippen's announcement that his wife had died in California only set tongues wagging all the faster.

Then one July morning, Chief Inspector Walter Dew of Scotland Yard and another detective knocked on Crippen's door. But the good doctor and his love had already fled in a panic. The detectives proceeded to ransack the house for clues, even digging up the flower garden and greenhouse. Two full days of investigation yielded nothing. But Dew could not shake the feeling that something was amiss in one dank corner of the house, a basement coal room.

Dew returned on the third day and, armed with a stove poker, began probing the brick floor of the coal room. He pried up some loose bricks, and when he shoveled the underlying earth away, a sickening stench drove him out into the garden. Fortified by a gulp of brandy, Dew returned to the cellar to identify the remains of a human torso wrapped in a man's pajama top. The head, arms, and legs were missing. The trunk of the body had been carefully filleted so as to remove all bones. Later analysis revealed the remains to contain traces of hyoscine hydrobromide, a poison derived from a species of the deadly nightshade family.

Newspaper headlines screamed out the grisly details of the case, as Scotland Yard mounted a massive search for Crippen, who was suspected to be traveling in the company of LeNeve.

London's *Weekly Dispatch* emblazoned a headline with the Crippen hunt in 1910.

Meanwhile, back on the *Montrose* steaming for Canada, Capt. Kendall faced a dilemma. The ship was one of the first such liners to be equipped with Guglielmo Marconi's recent invention, wireless radio. But the transmitter only had a range of 150 miles. Kendall needed to decide soon if his suspicions were correct and act quickly.

He spent a restless night mulling over the situation, then rose the next morning and handed the radio operator a message to relay to the ship's owners in Liverpool: "Have strong suspicions that Crippen London cellar murderer and accomplice are among saloon passengers. Moustache taken off, growing beard, accomplice dressed as a boy. Voice manner and build undoubtedly a girl. Both traveling as Mr. and Master Robinson."

Within hours Inspector Dew had boarded the *Laurentic*, a much faster steamer also bound for Quebec. Despite the three-day lead, with luck the vessel could beat the *Montrose* to Canada. Over the course of the following week millions of newspaper readers on both sides of the Atlantic followed Dew's desperate race to apprehend a murderer, while the Robinsons enjoyed their cruise, oblivious that their identities were public knowledge.

Early Sunday morning, July 31, the *Montrose* lay at anchor off the mouth of the St. Lawrence River. A pilot boat carrying Dew and a party of Canadian police knifed across the water. Dew immediately made his way to the bridge and shook hands with Kendall, who pointed out the elder Robinson on the deck below.

As Dew approached, the fugitive raised his bulgy eyes and then only a few feet away Dew said, "Good morning, Dr. Crippen." Dew never forgot the sudden twitching of Crippen's Adam's apple as he realized the jig was up.

Manacled and led to a state room, Crippen did not

hear the woman's shriek five minutes later as Dew burst into Ethel's room and arrested her while reading in bed. Then a horde of reporters bounded over the sides of the Montrose, and began collecting scraps of information from passengers for the millions of anxious readers who awaited the outcome of Crippen's trans-Atlantic flight.

Those readers found plenty to interest them over the course of the next three months as the case against the first criminal to be apprehended via the wireless proceeded in London. Crippen maintained his innocence to the end to no avail. Belle's remains were positively identified through an appendectomy scar. Originally charged as an accessory, Ethel won acquittal when it was proved that she knew nothing of the murder. But Crippen met his fate on the gallows on November 23, 1910, protesting his innocence to the end.

Over the course of succeeding decades the Crippen case has been immortalized in scores of books. In 1961, it formed the basis for a none too successful musical by Wolf Markowitz and Monty Normal, *Belle, or the Ballad of Dr. Crippen.* Alfred Hitchcock acknowledged that the Crippen murder inspired his classic film *Rear Window,* starring James Stewart and Grace Kelly.

Now, the waxen image of the murderer who brought attention to Coldwater continues to stare out at the thousands who tour the Chamber of Horror at Madame Tussaud's Museum in London.

SOURCES

Potawatomi Tears

Barber, Edward W. "Beginnings in Eaton County: Its Earliest Settlements and Settlers," *Michigan Pioneer Collection.* Vol. 29 (1899-1900). p. 335.

Baroux, Louis. *An Early Indian Mission.* Berrien Springs, 1976.

Clifton, James A., Cornell, George L. and McClurken, James M. *People of the Three Fires...*Grand Rapids, (1986).

(Durant, Samuel). *History of Kalamazoo County, Michigan.* Philadelphia, 1880.

Hulst, Cornelia Steketee. *Indian Sketches...*New York, 1912.

(Johnson, Crisfield). *History of Branch County, Michigan.* Philadelphia, 1879.

Hulst, Cornelia Steketee. *History of Hillsdale County, Michigan.* Philadelphia, 1879.

Manassah, Sallie. *A History of the Nottawasippe Huron Band of the Potawatomi Indians.* Battle Creek, 1983.

McKee, Irving, ed. *The Trail of Death: Letters of Benjamin Marie Petit.* Indiana Historical Society Publication. Vol. 14, No. 1. 1941.

Neumeyer, Elizabeth A. *Indian Removal in Michigan, 1833-1855.* Masters Thesis. Central Michigan University. June, 1968.

Neumeyer, Elizabeth. "Michigan Indians Battle Against Removal," *Michigan History.* Vol. LV, No. 4. (Winter 1971). p. 275.

Neumeyer, Elizageth, ed. "A Michigan 'Trail of Tears': The Holcomb Reminiscence," *Heritage Battle Creek.* Vol. 1 (Fall 1991). p. 54.

Quimby, George Irving. *Indian Life in the Upper Great Lakes.* Chicago, (1960).

Schoolcraft, Henry Rowe. *Historical...Information Respecting the Indian Tribes...*6 vols. Philadelphia, 1851-1857.

St. Dominic Original Indian Souvenir. N. P. (ca. 1910).

Supplementary Memorial of Certain Indians Residing in Michigan and Indiana. 42nd congress, 2nd Session. House of Representatives Miscellaneous Document No. 137. March 19, 1872.

Thomas, James M., compiler. *Kalamazoo County Directory with a History of the County.* Kalamazoo, 1869.

Tiedke, Kenneth E. *A Study of the Hannahville Indian Community.* Michigan State College Agricultural

Experiment Station Special Bulletin 369. (April 1951).
Trigger, Bruce C., ed. *Handbook of North American Indians*.
Vol. 15 *Northeast*. Washington, 1978.
Weissert, Charles A. *An Account of Southwest Michigan and
Berrien County*. Vol. III of *Historic Michigan* by George
N. Fuller. National Historical Association, (1926).

Pioneers in Petticoats
Baird, Elizabeth Therese. "Reminiscences of Early Days on
Mackinac Island," *Collections of the State Historical
Society of Wisconsin.* Vol XIV (1898). p. 17.
Bristol, Mary Ann Brevoort. "Reminiscences of the
Northwest," *Collections of the State Historical Society of
Wisconsin.* Vol VIII (1879). p. 293.
Dye, Mrs. Richard. "Coming to Michigan," *Michigan
Pioneer Collections.* Vol VIII (1886). p. 260.
Ellet, Elizabeth F. *Pioneer Women of the West*. New York,
1852.
Kirkland, Caroline Matilda. *A New Home—Who'll Follow?*
Reprint with introduction by William S. Osborne. New
Haven, Conn., (1965).
"Mrs. Nancy Howard, of Port Huron, and Her Interesting
Recollections," *Michigan Pioneer Collections.* Vol XIV
(1889). p. 532.
Riddell, William R. *The Life of William Dummer
Powell*...Lansing, 1924.
Schettler, Eliza M. Scott. "Lights and Shadows From Pioneer
Life," *Michigan Pioneer Collections.* Vol XXXV (1907).
p. 184.
Withey, Mrs. S. L. "Personal Recollections of the Early Days
of Richland and Grand Rapids," *Michigan Pioneer
Collections.* Vol. V (1884). p. 434.

Whitefish Point: Graveyard of the Great Lakes
Allen, James. *Expedition to the Northwest Indians...in 1832.*
Washington, 1834.
Bowen, Dana Thomas. *Shipwrecks of the Lakes.* Daytona
Beach, Florida, 1952.
Carter, James L. and Rankin, Ernest H., eds. *North to Lake
Superior: The Journal of Charles W. Penny.* Marquette,
1970.
Disturnell, J. *Sailing on the Great Lakes*...Philadelphia, 1874.
Gilman, Chandler R. *Life on the Lakes*...2 vols. N. Y., 1836.
Hyde, Charles K. *The Northern Lights: Lighthouses of the
Upper Great Lakes.* Lansing, 1986.

Kellogg, Louise Phelps, ed. *Early Narratives of the Northwest 1634-1699.* N. Y., 1917.

Lamb, Martha J. "The American Life Saving Service," *Harper's Monthly.* Vol. LVIV (February, 1882). p. 357.

Mason, Philip P., ed. *Schoolcraft's Expedition to Lake Itasca.* East Lansing, 1958.

McKenney, Thomas L. *Sketches of a Tour to the Lakes...*Baltimore, 1827.

Nute, Grace Lee. "The American Fur Company's Fishing Enterprises On Lake Superior," *Mississippi Valley Historical Review.* Vol. XII, No. 4 (March 1926). p. 483.

Nute, Grace Lee. *Lake Superior.* Indianapolis, (1944).

Perrault, Jean Baptiste. "Narrative of the Travels and Adventures of a Merchant Voyageur..." *Michigan Pioneer Collections.* Vol. 37 (1909-1910). p. 508.

Peters, Bernard C., ed. *Lake Superior Journal: Bela Hubbard's Account of the 1840 Houghton Expedition.* Marquette, 1983.

Ripley, James M. "Whitefish Point Light," *Inland Seas.* Vol. 24, No. 4 (Winter 1968). p. 270.

Schoolcraft, Henry Rowe. *Narrative Journal of Travels...in the Year 1820.* Albany, 1821.

Stonehouse, Frederick. *Lake Superior's "Shipwreck Coast."* (Au Train, Michigan, 1985).

Williams, Mentor L. "Horace Greeley Tours the Great Lakes," *Inland Seas.* Vol. 3, No. 3 (July 1947). p. 137.

Wolff, Julius F., Jr. *Lake Superior Shipwrecks.* (Duluth, 1990).

Memories of Michigan Medics

Buley, R. Carlyle. *The Old Northwest: Pioneer Period 1815-1840.* 2 Vols. Bloomington, Illinois, (1950).

Burr, C. B., ed. *Medical History of Michigan.* 2 Vols. Minneapolis, 1930.

Carney, James T., ed. *Berrien Bicentennial.* Stevensville, Michigan, 1976.

Dunbar, Willis. *Kalamazoo and How It Grew and Grew...*Faculty Contributions, Western Michigan University, 1969.

(Durant, Samuel W.) *History of Kalamazoo County, Michigan...*Philadelphia, 1880.

Evans, William A. "Michigan's Contribution to Early Roentgenology," *Journal of the Michigan State Medical Society.* May, 1934.

Garrison, Fielding H. *An Introduction to the History of*

Medicine...Philadelphia, 1929.

Historical Papers of the Kalamazoo Academy of Medicine. N.
P., (1976).

*History of Allegan and Barry Counties,
Michigan*...Philadelphia, 1880.

Holbrook, Stewart. *The Golden Age of Quackery.* N. Y.,
1959.

Massie, Larry B. and Schmitt, Peter J. *Kalamazoo: The Place
Behind the Product.* (Woodland Hills, California, 1981).

McNair, Rush. *Medical Memoirs of 50 Years In Kalamazoo.*
N. P., (1938).

Pickard, Madge E. and Buley, R. Carlyle. *The Midwest
Pioneer: His Ills, Cures and Doctors.* N. Y., 1946.

Swantek, Wanda. *The Sisters of St. Joseph of Nazareth, 1889-
1929, A Chronicle.* Nazareth, Mi., 1983.

Thomas, Henry F. *A Twentieth Century History of Allegan
County, Michigan.* Chicago, 1907.

Thomas, Nathan. *An Account of His Life Written by Himself.*
Cassopolis, 1925.

Van Buren, Anson De Puy. "The Fever and Ague...,"
Michigan Pioneer Collections. Vol. V (1882). p. 300

"World Beat a Path to Door of Niles Doctor," *Niles Daily
Star.* 25 March 1961.

Stalking Michigan's First Celery Grower

Beecher, Catherine. *Housekeeper's Receipt Book.* N. Y.,
1845.

Buist, Robert. *The Family Kitchen Gardener.* N. Y., (1847).

Child, Lydia. *The American Frugal Housewife.* Boston,
1835.

Dunbar, Willis. *Kalamazoo and How it Grew and
Grew*...Faculty Contributions, Western Michigan
University, 1969.

Dunbar, Willis. "Stories of Michigan—Kalamazoo Celery."
Script of Radio Program broadcast on WJEF, Grand
Rapids. Aug 13, 1947.

Fessenden, Thomas. *The New American Gardener.*
Cincinnati, 1834.

Ford, F. Rowe. *Kalamazoo the Debt Free City*...(Kalamazoo,
1939)

Garton, James. *The Practical Gardener and Gentlemen's
Directory for Every Month in the Year.* London, 1769.

Hedrick, U. P., ed. *Sturtevant's Notes on Edible Plants.*
Albany, 1919.

Homespun, Priscilla. *The Universal Receipt Book.*

Philadelphia, 1817.

Horst, Oscar. "The Decline of Celeryville," unpublished article.

Kalamazoo Gazette. 1890-1980.

"Kalamazoo Gazette, Centennial Edition." Kalamazoo, January 24, 1937.

Little, Frank. "Celery Culture at Kalamazoo, Michigan," *U. S. Department of Agriculture Annual Report.* 1886. p. 343.

Lucas, R. E. and Wittwer, S. H. *Celery Production in Michigan.* Michigan State University Extension Bulletin 339. N. D.

Massie, Larry B. and Schmitt, Peter J. *Kalamazoo: The Place Behind the Product.* (Woodland Hills, California, 1981).

McMahon, Bernard. *The American Gardener's Calendar.* Philadelphia, 1819.

Michigan. Bureau of Labor and Industrial Statistics. *17th Annual Report.* Lansing, 1900.

Michigan. Transactions of the State Agricultural Society...Lansing, 1850-1880. Title Varies.

Niven, Robert. *The Celery Culture.* The Rural Library. No. 7 (May, 1892). New York.

Trall, Russel. *New Hydropathic Cook-Book.* N. Y., 1853.

Van Bochove, G. *Kalamazoo Celery: Its Cultivation and Secret of Success.* Kalamazoo, 1893.

Wheeler, Eliza Ann. *The Frugal Housekeeper's Kitchen Companion.* N. Y., 1847.

Father Sifferath, Forgotten Missionary to the Ottawa

McClurken, James M. *Gah-Baeh-Jhagwah-Buk: The Way it Happened*...East Lansing, (1991).

Morley, Jan, ed. *Harbor Springs A Collection of Historical Essays.* Harbor Springs, 1981.

Pare, George. *The Catholic Church in Detroit 1701-1888.* Detroit, 1951.

Piling, James C. *Bibliography of the Algonquian Languages.* Washington, 1891.

Rezek, Antoine I. *History of the Diocese of Sault Ste. Marie and Marquette*...2 Vols. Houghton, Mi., 1906.

Shurtleff, Mary Belle. *Old Arbre Croche.* N. P., (1945).

Sifferath, Nicolas Louis. Collection. Includes records, correspondence, newspaper clippings, etc. Including his "Lecture on the Indians" in Archives of Nazareth, Michigan.

Sifferath, N. L. *A Short Compendium of the Catechism for*

*the Indians...*Buffalo, 1869.

Swantek, Wanda. "Life of Father Sifferath," unpublished article.

Swantek, Wanda. *The Sisters of St. Joseph of Nazareth, 1889-1929, A Chronicle.* Nazareth, 1983.

Verwyst, P. Chrisostomus. *Life and Labors of Rt. Rev. Frederic Baraga...*Milwaukee, 1900.

Walling, Regis M. and Rupp, N. Daniel, eds. *The Diary of Bishop Frederick Baraga First Bishop of Marquette, Michigan.* Detroit, 1990.

Wright, John C. *The Crooked Tree: Indian Legends.* Harbor Springs, 1917.

Wright, John C. *The Ottawan.* Lansing, 1895.

Civil War Belles and Battles

Dannett, Sylvia, ed. *Noble Women of the North.* N. Y., 1959.

Davis, Curtis Carroll. "Companions of Crisis: The Spy Memoir as a Social Document," *Civil War History.* Vol. 10, No. 4. (December 1964). p. 385.

Dictionary of American Biography. 21 Vols. N. Y., 1943.

Dietrich, Emily. "Laura Smith Haviland: Emancipator," in *Historic Women of Michigan: a Sesquicentennial Celebration.* Edited by Rosalie Riegle Troester. Lansing, (1987).

Edmonds, Sarah Emma. *Nurse and Spy in the Union Army.* Hartford, Connecticut, 1865.

Faust, Patricia, ed. *Historical Times Illustrated Encyclopedia of the Civil War.* N. Y., (1986).

Fladeland, Betty. "Alias Franklin Thompson," *Michigan History.* Vol. XLII (1958). p. 345.

Goodrich, Frank B. *The Tribute Book...*N. Y., 1865.

Harris, Fran. *Focus: Michigan Women 1701-1977.* Michigan Coordinating Committee of the National Commission on the Observance of Women's Year, 1977.

Haviland, Laura. *A Woman's Life Work.* Cincinnati, 1881.

History of Berrien and Van Buren Counties, Michigan. Philadelphia, 1880.

Holland, Mary A. *Our Army Nurses.* Boston, 1895.

Mann, Wayne. *Interview.* Kalamazoo, 1983.

Millbrook, Mrs. Raymond H., ed. *Michigan Women in the Civil War.* Michigan Civil War Centennial Observance Commission Publication, 1963.

Moore, Frank. *Women of the War; Their Heroism and Self Sacrifice.* Hartford, 1867.

Rickman, Irwin. "Pauline Cushman. She was a Heroine But

Not a Lady," *Civil War Times Illustrated*. February 1969. p. 39.

Robertson, John, ed. *Michigan in the War*. Lansing, 1882.

Sarmiento, F. L. *Life of Pauline Cushman, the Celebrated Union Spy and Scout*. Philadelphia, (1865).

Wood, Ann Douglas. "The War Within a War: Women Nurses in the Union Army," *Civil War History*. Vol. 3. (September 1972). p. 197.

When Passenger Pigeons Darkened Michigan Skies

Barrows, Walter Bradford. *Michigan Bird Life*. Lansing, 1912.

Bendire, Charles. *Life Histories of North American Birds*...Washington, 1892.

Case, William L. "Passing of the Passenger Pigeon," *Michigan History Magazine*. Vol. XIV. No. 2. (Spring, 1930). p. 262.

Cook, A. J. *Birds of Michigan*. Michigan Agricultural College Bulletin No. 94. East Lansing, 1893.

Hedrick, Ulysses P. *The Land of the Crooked Tree*. N. Y., 1948

Mershon, William B. *The Passenger Pigeon*. N. Y., 1907

Muir, John. *The Story of My Boyhood and Youth*. Boston, 1913

A Passing in Cincinnati September 1, 1914. Washington, 1976.

Pender, James. *History of Benton Harbor*. Chicago, 1915.

Rowland, O. W. *A History of Van Buren County Michigan*. 2 vols. Chicago, 1912.

Schorger, A. W. "The Great Wisconsin Passenger Pigeon Nesting of 1871," *Proceedings of the Linnaean Society of New York*. No. 48 (1936). p. 1.

Wilson, Etta S. "Personal Recollections of the Passenger Pigeon," *The Auk*. Vol. XI, No. 2. (April 1934). p. 157.

Wood, Norman A. *The Birds of Michigan*. Miscellaneous Publications Museum of Zoology, University of Michigan, No. 75. Ann Arbor, 1951.

From Gutter to Pulpit

Dutcher, George M. *Disinthralled: A Story of My Life*. Hartford, Conn., 1873.

Gough, John B. *Autobiography and Personal Recollections of*...Springfield, Mass., 1870.

Hess, Joseph F. *Out of Darkness Into Light; or, The Story of*

My Life. Toronto, Canada, (1890).
Knapp, Martin Wells. *Revival Tornadoes;* or *The Life and Labors of Rev. Joseph H. Weber, Evangelist.* Albion, Michigan, 1889.
Long, Mason. *The Life of...*10th edition. Fort Wayne, (1887).
Shockey, Samuel W. *Twenty-five Years Fighting Fate,* or *Thrilling Reminiscences of the Travels of* ...Boston, (1892).
Trainer, George Francis. *The Life and Adventures of Ben Hogan, the Wickedest Man in the World.* N. P., (1878).
Wills, Henry O. *Twice Born;* or *The Two Lives of* ...Cincinnati, 1890.
Wilson, James Grant and Fiske, John, eds. *Appleton's Cyclopedia of American Biography.* 6 vols. New York, 1888.

Michigan at the White City: The Columbian Exposition of 1893

Burg, David F. *Chicago's White City of 1893.* University Press of Kentucky. 1976.
Chicago Tribune Glimpses of the World's Fair. Chicago, 1893.
Flinn, John J. *Official Guide to the World's Columbian Exposition.* Chicago, 1893.
Michigan and Its Resources. Lansing, 1893.
Pokagon, Simon. *Queen of the Woods.* Hartford, Michigan. 3rd ed. 1901.
Stevens, Mrs. Mark. *Six Months at the World's Fair.* Detroit, 1895.
Weston, I. M., ed. *Report of the Board of World's Fair Managers for the State of Michigan.* Lansing, 1899.
World's Columbian Exposition. State of Michigan. *Rules and Regulations of the Board...*Flint, 1892.

"Get out and Get Under": Automotive Pioneers in Kalamazoo

Blood, Howard E. to Dennis Shattuck. 3 page letter describing career. 11 Jan. 1966.
Dolnar, Hugh. "Blood Brothers' Side Entrance Tonneau Touring Car," *Cycle and Automobile Trade Journal.* November 1904. p. 117.
Dunbar, Willis. *Kalamazoo and How it Grew...and Grew...*Faculty Contributions, Western Michigan University, 1969.

Fisher, David and Little, Frank, eds. *Compendium of History and Biography of Kalamazoo County, Michigan.* Chicago, (1906).

Georgano, G. N. *The Complete Encyclopedia of Motorcars 1885 to the Present.* N. Y., (1968).

"Greater Kalamazoo." Supplement to *Kalamazoo Daily Gazette,* July 30, 1904.

Kalamazoo City Directory. 1900-1910.

Kalamazoo Gazette. 1900-1914.

"Kalamazoo Gazette, Centennial Edition." Kalamazoo, January 24, 1937.

Kalamazoo Telegraph. 1900-1910.

Massie, Larry B. and Schmitt, Peter J. *Kalamazoo: The Place Behind the Product.* (Woodland Hills, California, 1981).

Michigan Bureau of Labor and Industrial Statistics. Annual Reports. Lansing, 1900-1911.

Crippen, Killer from Coldwater

Birkenhead, the Earl of. *Famous Trials of History.* N. Y., 1926.

Bovee, Seton. "Crippen Was 'Killer' of Century." *Coldwater Sentinel.* 27 June 1961.

City Directory Coldwater, Michigan. Coldwater, 1912.

Cramp, Arthur J. ed. *Nostrums and Quackery.* Vol. 1. Chicago, 1911.

Cullen, Tom. *The Mild Murderer.* Boston, (1977).

Homes, Nathanial, compiler. *An Illustrated City Directory of Coldwater, Mich. 1894.* Coldwater 1894.

Portrait and Biographical Album of Branch County, Michigan. Chicago, 1888.

INDEX

287

288

289

292

295

Larry B. Massie is a Michigan product and proud of it. Born in Grand Rapids in 1947, he grew up in Allegan. Following a tour in Viet Nam as a U. S. Army paratrooper, he worked as a telephone lineman, construction laborer, bartender and in a pickle factory before earning three degrees in history from Western Michigan University.

He honed his research skills during an eight-year position with the W. M. U. Archives and Regional History Collection. He left in 1983 to launch a career as a freelance historian, specializing in the heritage of the state he loves. An avid book collector, he lives with his wife and workmate Priscilla, and their 30, 000 volume library, in a rambling old schoolhouse nestled in the Allegan State Forest. Sons Adam, Wallie and Larry Jr., as well as Maggie, Skippy, Jiggs and Ossie, pets canine and feline, insure there is never a dull moment.

Larry B. Massie among the tools of the trade.

297

Larry and Priscilla Massie's

MICHIGAN HISTORY BOOKS AVAILABLE FROM THE PRISCILLA PRESS

Potawatomi Tears and Petticoat Pioneers 296 pages, ill. bib. index. $8.95

The Romance of Michigan's Past 270 pages, ill. bib. index. $8.95

Pig Boats and River Hogs 296 pages, ill. bib. index. $8.95

Copper Trails and Iron Rails 290 pages, ill. bib. index. $10.95

Voyages into Michigan's Past 298 pages, ill. bib. index. $10.95

From Frontier Folk to Factory Smoke 182 pages, ill. $8.95

Walnut Pickles and Watermelon Cake: A Century of Michigan Cookery 354 pages, 8 1/2 x 11, ill. bib. index, hardbound. $24.95

Warm Friends and Wooden Shoes:
An Illustrated History of Holland, Michigan 128 pages, 8 1/2 x 11, ill. bib. index, hardbound. $19.95

Shipping on individual books $1.50
Two or more books ordered retail—shipping is free
Michigan residents please add 4% sales tax

Order from Larry B. & Priscilla Massie
2109 41ST STREET
ALLEGAN FOREST, MICHIGAN
(616) 673-3633

Please indicate if you would like the author to inscribe the books.